About the author

Chris Rogers is Leverhulme Early Career Fellow
at the University of York. His first book, *The IMF
and European Economies: Crisis and Conditionality*,
was published in 2012. Chris is currently working
on a research project on the political economy of
mutual organization.

T0321546

CAPITALISM AND ITS ALTERNATIVES

Chris Rogers

Zed Books
LONDON

Capitalism and Its Alternatives was first published in 2014 by
Zed Books Ltd, 7 Cynthia Street, London N1 9JF, UK.

www.zedbooks.co.uk

Set in Monotype Plantin and FFKievit by Ewan Smith, London
Index: ed.emery@thefreeuniversity.net
Cover designed by Steven Marsden

A catalogue record for this book is available from the British Library
Library of Congress Cataloging in Publication Data available

ISBN 978-1-78032-737-2 hb
ISBN 978-1-78032-736-5 pb
ISBN 978-1-78032-738-9 pdf
ISBN 978-1-78032-739-6 epub
ISBN 978-1-78032-740-2 Kindle

CONTENTS

ACKNOWLEDGEMENTS

This book was written during a Leverhulme Early Career Fellowship (ECF-2011-003) and I am grateful to the Leverhulme Trust for the funding that allowed me to spend time thinking through the issues raised in the book. I would like to thank Ken Barlow at Zed Books for his help in developing the project in its early stages, as well as Werner Bonefeld, Charith Cabraal, Chris Clarke, Catia Gregoratti, Nicholas Larkman, Martin O'Neill, Adrienne Roberts, Carole Spary, Kika Sroka-Miller, Ted Svensson, Matthew Watson and anonymous referees, all of whom have provided extremely useful comments and observations, either during ongoing discussions about the subject matter of the book, or on earlier drafts. All of these suggestions and discussions have contributed to improving the final text. The support and encouragement of friends and family while I was writing the book are, as ever, greatly appreciated. Finally, I would like to thank Ian Paten for his hard work in copy-editing the manuscript.

INTRODUCTION: CAPITALISM AND ITS ALTERNATIVES

Introduction

The collapse of sub-prime mortgage markets, which led to the failure of some financial institutions, the bailout of others, and the subsequent recession, has had profound implications. In Europe, both Greece and Spain have seen unemployment reach unprecedented heights of over 25 per cent. In May 2013, youth unemployment Europe-wide was 23.1 per cent; in Greece it was as high as 59.2 per cent and in Spain 56.5 per cent (Eurostat 2013). The focus on the sovereign debt positions of many states, especially Portugal, Italy, Ireland, Greece and Spain, has exacerbated these problems as public sector employment has been cut alongside welfare budgets. However, it is not just the peripheral European economies which have been affected, as unemployment in the United Kingdom and the United States has reached levels of 8 per cent and 7.5 per cent respectively (ibid.). Like Portugal, Italy, Ireland, Greece and Spain, the United Kingdom and the United States have both used austerity as one of the primary forms of crisis response, and a recent report estimated that austerity will have come at a cost of 2 million American jobs by 2019 (CAP 2013).

The consequences of the global financial crisis have therefore been felt acutely at a social level throughout Europe and the world. In light of the fact that the crisis originated with the imprudent behaviour of financial actors, and the fact that costs associated with the crisis have been socialized in the form of unemployment and welfare retrenchment, it is perhaps unsurprising that there has been an upsurge of discontent about the way in which the capitalist system operates. This has been clearly manifested in the form of the Occupy movement, which has been one of the primary modes of resistance to the prevailing form of capitalism through its occupations of public spaces in New York, London and elsewhere. Discontent about how the benefits of the capitalist system are distributed has been clearly manifested in the slogan that it has popularized: 'we are the 99 per cent'.

The global financial crisis of the late 2000s, the distribution of the benefits of the way the system operated, and the distribution of the costs of the way it was saved, provide strong reasons to think about whether capitalism is a desirable form of social and economic organization. However, this reasoning is amplified by the fact that it is not the first time that the capitalist system has found itself in crisis. In the 1930s, the Great Depression led to widespread unemployment that provoked international economic competition and contributed to the onset of the Second World War. This represented the ultimate socialization of the costs of capitalist failure; as John Holloway (1995: 21) phrased it, after the Great Depression and the Second World War 'capital could deal again and, over the bodies of twenty million people, a fresh game could start'. In the 1970s, the global economy once again found itself in crisis as many countries were faced with rises in unemployment occurring along with stagnant growth – the phenomenon of stagflation. While the crisis did not lead to war as it did in the interwar period, the 1970s stagflation nonetheless resulted in widespread cuts in welfare that meant people were exposed even further to the rigours of the marketplace. As such, if the market could not provide them with employment, people had increasingly less to fall back on for their well-being.

Although periods of vast economic growth, such as the years immediately following the Second World War and the 1990s and early 2000s, have suggested that 'such episodes have finally been overcome, and the cycles of boom and bust banished, these hopes have always turned out in the end to be illusory' (Gamble 2009: 6). As responses to previous crises have not appeared to generate greater or longer-lasting stability, the rationale for asking questions about the origins of crises in capitalism and potential solutions to them could not be stronger. In light of this rationale, this book asks four questions about capitalism. First, it asks how wealth is created and used in capitalism, and what role the state plays in facilitating the creation of wealth. Secondly, it asks how capitalism is related to crisis, and specifically, whether capitalism displays an *inherent tendency towards crisis* that ultimately means an alternative system of organization is required if stability is to be achieved. Thirdly, the book asks what kind of alternative systems of organization might be realized, and what their consequences could be. Finally, the book asks how individuals and groups of individuals could create such an alternative form of social organization.

A note on terminology The book will draw on four core concepts. The first of these is *capitalism*. The term *capitalism* is used throughout the book to refer to the prevailing form of social organization. While acknowledging that the ways in which capitalism operates and the implications of these operations are contested, this book defines capitalism in terms of one commonly accepted distinguishing feature: that capitalism is a system that organizes the production, distribution and exchange of goods, on the basis of private property, with a view to realizing profit and therefore increasing wealth. The second term is *alternative capitalism*, which is used to describe a system where the capitalistic relationship between state and market is re-regulated, but not fundamentally reformed, in order to try to produce optimal social and economic outcomes. The aim of an *alternative capitalism* is to maximize wealth and profit by introducing a different structure of rules to govern capitalism. The third concept is that of an *alternative to capitalism*. An alternative *to* capitalism is distinct from capitalism because it places an emphasis on social and civic goals, rather than purely focusing on pecuniary gain. In contrast to capitalism, an alternative *to* capitalism is founded on collective or community property rights, rather than individual property rights, although the form and extent of collective or community property rights may vary. Where the book is referring to either an alternative capitalism or an alternative *to* capitalism, it uses the form 'alternative (to) capitalism'. The final concept the book uses is *anti-capitalism*. It uses the term anti-capitalism to refer to the act of resisting capitalism, whether this occurs by attempting to influence the state, taking control of the state, or actions taken independently or outside of the state. An individual who pursues or wishes to pursue an alternative *to* capitalism can therefore be described as an anti-capitalist.

Traditions of resistance

In its consideration of capitalism and its alternatives, this book accepts that it is possible to perceive capitalism and its consequences in different ways. Furthermore, it acknowledges that the way in which capitalism and its consequences are perceived will have a fundamental impact on whether people deem capitalism to be desirable, whether they would prefer an alternative capitalism or an alternative *to* capitalism, and therefore whether they believe that it is important and worthwhile engaging in resistance to capitalism through the social act of anti-capitalism. However, the central argument of this book is that capitalism displays intrinsic tendencies towards crisis that make an alternative *to* capitalism desirable, and so justifies anti-capitalist action. In doing so, it argues that capitalism is a product of social interaction between people, and that it is remade or resisted through our social action. This emphasis on social constitution challenges common assertions about the inevitability of capitalist logic, and in the process shows that the prospect of realizing an alternative to capitalism is more than wishful thinking.

In its discussions of alternatives to capitalism, however, this book guards against thinking of alternative forms of social organization as outcomes or utopias. Rather, it shows how various forms of alternative social and economic organization have shown a tendency to degenerate over time, or to reproduce injustices of capitalist social relations. It therefore suggests that alternatives to capitalism should be thought of as *processes* that need to be continually made and remade if they are not to degenerate or reproduce the injustices of capitalist social relations, and if desirable outcomes are to be realized. Reflecting the book's emphasis on the social constitution of economy and society, it rejects 'top-down' attempts to impose an alternative to capitalism by political means, and argues that anti-capitalist action should take a 'bottom-up' form, which requires democratic and pluralistic experimentation with different models of social and economic organization to expand the space in which non-capitalist activity takes place.

The arguments of the book therefore fit with a long tradition of anti-capitalist resistance. One of the most well-known instances of this kind of resistance was the insurrections of 1968, typified by the student revolts in Paris in May of that year. However, as Michael Watts (2001: 167) noted, the events of 1968 were far more than a local phenomenon; over seventy countries 'had major student actions during that year [and between] October 1967 and July 1968 there were over 2000 incidents world wide of student protest alone'. Furthermore, it was not just students engaged in the act of protest, the act of anti-capitalism. According to Watts' (ibid.: 167) study, 'if one were to add the related worker and other nonstudent demonstrations each country in the world would, on average, have had over 20 "incidents" over the nine-month period'. Nor was the substance of the protest uniform; 1968 had what Watts (ibid.: 171–2) has described as its Eastern, Western and Southern moments. In the first, typified by the Prague Spring and the Cultural Revolution in China, the focus of protests was anti-bureaucratic, and directed against the 'Old Left' and the corruption people perceived in it. In the second, typified by student protests in Paris and Berkeley, the focus of protests was opposition to consumerism and the pursuit of civil and social rights. In the third, the focus was the rejection of authority in the first generation of independent states in Africa and Latin America, where military dictatorship had displaced democratic rule.

Luc Boltanski (2002: 6) also highlights the diversity of the 1968 movement by distinguishing between its social and artistic critiques, where the former focused on inequality and poverty stemming from capitalism, and the latter on liberation, individual autonomy and authenticity. Michael Löwy (2002: 95) links this distinction between the social and artistic critique of capitalism to romanticism, which he defines as 'rebellion against modern capitalist society, in the name of past or premodern social and cultural values, as a protest against the modern disenchantment of the world'. Therefore the significance of 1968 can be seen not just across space, but also as a reflection of long-established traditions of resistance to prevailing social, political and economic forms or organization. On such readings, the events of 1968 can be interpreted as a demonstration of long-standing anti-capitalist feeling that rested on a critique of the world we live in and the injustices it creates, and in turn motivated action in order to try to address them.

Nonetheless, on other readings, the impact of 1968 has been vastly overstated. As Watts (2001: 163–4) has noted, history has not been kind to the 1960s. Critics on the left have viewed the anti-capitalist actions of that decade as a failed political project, a political project that did not realize its ambitions to move towards a more just form of social and economic organization. Critics on the right, on the other hand, have viewed the anti-capitalist actions of the 1960s as a successful cultural revolution, which was indicative of the decay of commonly accepted social values. On this basis, rather than producing radical outcomes, it has been argued that the anti-capitalism of the 1960s justified conservatism:

> Whether the voices emanate from London or Paris or New York or Mexico City, the death narrative reigns supreme [...] Sunil Khilani [...] sees the events of 1968 in France as a gesture of pure 'nothingness', 'made by and for intellectuals' [...] The Year 1968 was, in sum, nothing at all [...] It was a sort of grand fiesta of bullshit. (Ibid.: 166)

Even where the anti-capitalism of the late 1960s has been seen as more coherent than this, as more than 'a grand fiesta of bullshit', it has been criticized for its eventual conservatism. Luc Boltanski (2002: 10), for instance, has argued that the social critique of 1968 was muted because the leaders of workers' movements were eventually satisfied by small changes to the way that work and social life were organized. In particular, he notes how some members of the movement were 'even integrated themselves into the new mechanisms of power, in support of the Socialist government in France' (ibid.: 10). Thus, the significance of anti-capitalist action in the 1960s was capitalism's 'ability to turn around and render obsolete the constraints once relevant in the framework of the second spirit of capitalism', which laid the foundations for the 'redeployment of capitalism in the 1980s' (ibid.: 10).

In the longer term, then, it has been suggested that the legacy of 1968 was the creation of two political 'lefts', both of them modest. On the one hand, it created an anti-capitalist left that continued to engage in a social critique of economic relations by demanding new rights for those impoverished by capitalism, but seeks little more than a compromise between capitalism's need for flexibility and labourers' demands for job security. On the other, it created a left that seeks reform of interpersonal relations in terms of 'the generation and reproduction of human beings and of kinship relations', but is not anti-capitalist (ibid.: 13–15). Neither appears to represent a substantial or meaningful challenge to the prevailing form of social and economic organization. However, the events of the late 1960s were significant in at least two senses. First, they showed that people are willing and able to ask important questions about society and to express their discontent by taking action (Watts 2001: 160). Secondly, and perhaps more importantly, the events occurred during the pinnacle of the expansion of post-war liberal capitalism, and were not the product of a capitalist crisis as such (ibid.: 162; Löwy 2002: 96). This suggests that resistance to capitalism is constantly simmering beneath the surface as an expression of a generalized discontent with the implications of the prevailing form of social and economic organization, and that anti-capitalism is more than a fleeting moment associated with undesirable yet historically specific circumstances such as unemployment or rising inflation.

These notions that the anti-capitalism of 1968 either represented 'pure nothingness' or resulted in a compromised and co-opted political left can clearly be challenged by the persistence of anti-capitalist activity throughout the world. There are many such examples, which include action by indigenous movements seeking to protect their land from appropriation by the state. This is typified by the Zapatista resistance to the North American Free Trade Agreement in Mexico (Cuninghame 2008), which has gathered support far beyond the Zapatista communities themselves, as they have been able to use communications technologies in order to 'get their message out despite governmental spin and censorship' (Cleaver 2008: 130). Alongside other organized activities, the ability of the Zapatista movement to raise awareness of its struggle has 'facilitated discussions and debate among concerned observers that led to the organization of protest and support activities in over forty countries around the world' (ibid.: 130). Despite claims that the anti-capitalism of the 1960s was a failure, such movements show that people are still willing to question the capitalist system and to try to create an alternative. On a smaller scale, organizations like the Starbucks Workers Campaign have shown a similar willingness to question the prevailing form of social and economic organization, by challenging the notion of progressive capitalism (Shukaitis 2008: 104). Some of the anti-capitalist actions featuring prominently in the media have included the Battle of Seattle against the World Trade Organization, and the 2009 protests against the G20 in London, but there have been many more besides (see Tormey 2004: 177–9 for a timeline). All of these varying forms of ongoing struggle indicate people's continued willingness to question capitalism, ponder alternatives, and consider how they might be realized.

One of the most enduring forums in which this tradition of resistance can be seen is the World Social Forum, which has brought together civil society organizations every year since 2001 in order to discuss and debate the possibilities for an alternative future. According to its charter,

> The World Social Forum is an open meeting place for reflective thinking, democratic debate of ideas, formulation of proposals, free exchange of experiences and interlinking for effective action, by groups and movements of civil society that are opposed to neo-liberalism and to domination of the world by capital and any form of imperialism, and are committed to building a planetary society directed towards fruitful relationships among Humankind and between it and the Earth. (World Social Forum 2013)

Rather than operating as a body, the World Social Form emerged in a decentralized fashion to join organizations that share its common aims. According to Isabelle Biagiotti (2004: 533), the important thing about the World Social Forum is that the diverse range of participants have the opportunity to meet each other: 'In the words of Chico Whitaker, one of the founders of the Forum, the aspiration is to create "a space" and not "a movement".'

However, this form of action by anti-capitalists has not always been easy for people to understand. For instance, the 2004 World Social Forum in Mumbai was criticized by some media outlets on the grounds that its breadth of coverage meant that it did not have a message (Becker 2007: 209); 'All WSF observers, especially the media, have remarked on the heterogeneous and "illegible" character of the Forum' (Biagiotti 2004: 537). However, as Whitaker noted, this is also precisely the point of the World Social Forum (see ibid.: 533; also Becker 2007: 209). According to Boaventura de Sousa Santos (2008: 252), the perceived weaknesses of the World Social Forum, which lie in its 'inability to discriminate among alternatives', are not something that can be 'separated from its strength – the celebration of diversity as value in itself'. As such, the idealism of the World Social Forum manifests itself in a negative sense as a critique of the world in which we live, rather than through the imagination of a world that may be, asserting only that 'another world is possible' (ibid.: 253). While it is the case that politicians have tried to take advantage of the World Social Forum, for instance in 2006, when Hugo Chávez argued that 'the forum should take advantage of its platform to build a political struggle' by supporting socialist governments (Becker 2007: 214), the Forum has eschewed the political on the grounds that the 'twentieth century proved with immense cruelty that to take power is not enough, that rather than taking power it is necessary to transform power' (De Sousa Santos 2008: 256).

The most recent manifestation of resistance in this form has come through the Occupy movement. As Fabian Balardini (2012: 35) has noted, 2011 saw a wave of protests throughout the Middle East and Africa, before being followed on 'October 15 by one of the largest global protests against economic and social injustice in history, throughout 951 cities in 82 countries. This worldwide protest was part of a growing global uprising known as the Occupy movement that had begun less than a month earlier in New York City.'

The Occupy movement is a diverse, democratic and non-hierarchical movement that came together 'in solidarity to express a feeling of mass injustice' derived from the fact that 'the future of the human race requires the cooperation of its members; that our system must protect our rights, and upon corruption of that system, it is up to the individuals to protect their own rights and those of their neighbours' (Occupy Wall Street 2011: 1).

Noam Chomsky (2012: 33) has noted how, through Alan Greenspan, the American establishment had acknowledged that the success of the neoliberal economy relied on the insecurity of workers, suggesting that Greenspan's view of the economy rested on the recognition that 'If working people are insecure, if they're part of what we now call the "precariat", living precarious existences, they're not going to make demands, they're not going to try to get wages, they won't get benefits'. As a result, it would be possible for the economic elite to 'kick 'em out if we don't need 'em'. Ultimately, it was through irony that Chomsky revealed his exasperation at the situation: 'And that's what's called a "healthy" economy, technically. And [Greenspan] was very highly praised for this, greatly admired.'

Rather than meandering towards irrelevance, the critique of capitalism, consideration of alternatives, and the means through which they might be realized have remained important, and have arguably become more important over time. As Naomi Klein (2011: 1–2) noted, Occupy appears stronger than the protests of the late 1990s that targeted various summits throughout the world because those protests were necessarily transient, and because they occurred at the peak of an economic boom. In contrast, she illustrates how the permanent physical presence of occupations allowed the movement to 'grow roots', and how the crisis that began in 2007 and 2008 made 'taking on an economic system based on greed' less of a 'tough sell'.

Like the anti-capitalist movements of the 1960s and the World Social Forum, the Occupy movement has not been without detractors seeking to highlight flaws that create an appearance of irrelevance. It has been suggested that knowing precisely what the 'Occupy movement is about is difficult to discern because of its internationally anarchic and leaderless composition', which makes it appear 'less like orchestrated change and more like "rebel without a cause"' (Boydston 2010: 20). As a result, critics have asked how far Occupy represents more than 'the politics of spectacle', and how it can be a sustainable movement over the medium to long term (Gamson and Sifry 2013: 159–63). Such commentators effectively question, in the same way as critics questioned 1968, how Occupy's anti-capitalist action can ever be more than *another* 'grand fiesta of bullshit'.

For some, the answer to this question is 'a little leadership' (Boydston 2010: 23). However, for others, the decentralized nature of the Occupy movement is not a fundamental flaw. Marianne Malinov (2013: 207), for instance, has suggested that the decentralized nature

of the movement allows it to act as 'a low-risk social change labora-
tory, birthing exciting new innovations in the form of organizing
tools, strategies, and hubs of Occupy-led or inspired alliances that
are building towards structural change'. For instance, she notes how
programmes like Occupy Our Homes in Minnesota have served to
institutionalize resistance to foreclosure by providing best-practice
advice to those threatened with repossession (ibid.: 208–9). Likewise,
she notes how Drop the Swap in Oakland, California, has been able
to unite the local council, unions and community groups, in order
to lobby Goldman Sachs to drop predatory financial contracts after
it received relief from the federal government, and failed to pass
the benefits on to cities (ibid.: 211). Globally then, it can be argued
that the decentralized actions of the Occupy movement 'are greater
than the sum of their parts [and] are components of what is emerging in Occupy into a longer-term effort aimed at systemic change'
(ibid.: 213).

At various stages throughout the post-war period there have been
clearly defined anti-capitalist movements that have formed on the
basis of dissatisfaction with the prevailing form of social and economic relations, and sought to realize change by taking action. At
each of these stages, anti-capitalist action has prompted detractors
to try to highlight the ineffective nature of their resistance or their
irrelevance to 'big picture' questions on the grounds that they have
often been on a small scale. Nonetheless, the persistence of anti-
capitalist action from 1968 through to Occupy clearly suggests that
the critique of capitalism, considerations of alternative forms of
organization, and the ways in which they might be realized remain
pressing issues in contemporary society. It is the purpose of this book
to introduce and engage with various approaches to these endeavours.
In doing so, it argues that capitalism is an inherently crisis-prone
form of social organization, which provides a clear rationale for an
alternative to capitalism; it argues that alternative forms of social
organization exist and the space in which they exist can be expanded;
and it argues that because the world in which we live is socially
constituted, such alternatives can be realized through democratic
and pluralistic 'bottom-up' social action.

The next chapter introduces four different theories of capitalism –

those of Adam Smith, Karl Marx, John Maynard Keynes and Friedrich Hayek. These theorists have produced some of the most important ideas in the history of political economy, which have had significant influence on the form that capitalism's institutional arrangements have taken. Smith was one of the fathers of political economy analysis, and his ideas played an important role in shaping the laissez-faire liberal state forms of the nineteenth and early twentieth centuries, while Karl Marx was his leading and most significant critic. In the post-war period, Keynes' understanding of capitalism played a central role in informing the construction of the institutions of the embedded-liberal world order that lasted from 1945 to the 1970s, while the ideas of Hayek were significant in shaping the neoliberal transformation in the late 1970s and 1980s. In sum, therefore, the ideas of these political economists have had a profound impact in shaping the way in which capitalism is understood, which has in turn shaped the institutional arrangements that govern it.

The purpose of the chapter is to show that capitalism is a contested concept, and its core argument is that our ideas about what capitalism is and what consequences it has play a fundamental role in shaping our judgements about whether an alternative (to) capitalism is desirable. For instance, it shows how Smith's conception of value suggests equality in the exchange relation, while Marx's conception of value emphasizes exploitation and class conflict. Similarly, it shows how Keynes believed that tendencies towards depression in the economy could be offset through state intervention, while Hayek believed that the only institution capable of promoting stability was the market itself. Given the diversity of these views about the processes that produce and manage the production of wealth in capitalism, it is clear that each will produce different understandings about how state, economy and society should be organized. In short, our ideas about and understanding of capitalism will shape our beliefs about whether or not it should be remade or resisted.

Despite these differences, these political economists share in common a view of state, economy and society, as forms of the way in which people interact with one another. The state and the economy are not seen as separate and externally related 'things' that have an existence outside the social interactions between people, which come to constitute them. This is significant because if it is accepted that the institutional structures of politics and economics are the products of interactions between people, it is possible to negate claims that there is no alternative to a particular course of action. This, in turn, opens up the possibility of creating alternative forms of organization through social action. The chapter's emphasis on the social constitution of state, economy and society provides the book with an analytical framework that informs but can also stand apart from the normative claims it develops later; *because our understanding of capitalism (and/or its alternatives) informs our actions which serve to create and re-create capitalism (and/or its alternatives), it is fundamentally important to reflect on capitalism (and/or its alternatives) if we are ever to live in the kind of world that we want to live in.*

Chapter 2 builds on this analytical framework and begins to develop the book's normative argument by considering the relationship between capitalism and crisis. It shows how the institutional arrangements broadly advocated by the political economy of Adam Smith, John Maynard Keynes and Friedrich Hayek have each been realized in the laissez-faire, embedded-liberal and neoliberal periods of the interwar period, the post-war period and the post-1979 period respectively. Through a historical examination of the interwar collapse and the Great Depression, the break-up of the Bretton Woods system and the 1970s stagflation, and the sub-prime mortgage crisis and the Great Recession, the chapter argues that these understandings of capitalism and the institutional arrangements they suggest fail to offer a convincing account of crises in capitalism or a basis for stability.

The implications of this analysis are extremely significant for developing a rationale for an alternative (to) capitalism. This is because if the institutional arrangements that logically flow from these understandings of capitalist social relations have been realized, and yet not served to create stability, these crises – in isolation – represent an important contribution to a critique of those particular understandings of capitalism. However, in combination these crises suggest something more profound about capitalism: that it is *intrinsically* unstable and crisis-prone. The chapter therefore returns to Marx, who believed that capitalism is fundamentally contradictory because it relies both on capitalists' need to lower wages to maintain profits in the face of competition, and the need to reproduce living labour, on which the creation of value and the accumulation of wealth depend. Chapter 2 therefore argues that it is not the *form* that capitalism takes – the particular ways in which people amass stocks of monetary wealth by pursuing profit – but *capitalism itself* which is at the root of crises. In other words, the chapter argues that it is treating the accumulation of stocks of wealth through the pursuit of profit as an important *end in itself* which is the source of instability and crises in capitalism. The chapter therefore establishes an empirical critique of the varying forms that capitalism has taken, which contributes to a theoretical critique of capitalism itself and provides a strong normative case for an alternative (to) capitalism.

Having established a strong normative case for an alternative (to) capitalism, the book turns its attention to the form that such an alternative might take in Chapter 3. In light of the fact that the previous forms capitalism has taken – the laissez-faire liberal, Keynesian and neoliberal – do not exhaust the possibilities for organizing capitalism in different ways, the chapter begins by considering the prospects of a libertarian alternative capitalism. This would see the state prioritize the protection of freedom and private property, but refrain from intervention in other areas. However, the chapter argues that libertarian positions are reliant on questionable assumptions about the basis of private property, and that even if these assumptions could be justified theoretically, the inequalities likely to result from these arrangements would foster discontent and ultimately prove unsustainable as a form of social and economic organization.

The chapter then considers cooperative and socialist alternatives to capitalism. It argues that these alternative forms of social organization, which incorporate principles of communal ownership to greater or lesser degrees, appear to have the potential to address the crisis dynamics of capitalism identified in the preceding chapter because they do not treat the accumulation of wealth as a desirable end point in itself. However, it also notes that historical attempts to create cooperative communities have encountered a number of practical obstacles, while the notion that there is only one form of socialism that would be desired by and beneficial for all individuals is illusory. In particular, it highlights how workers' movements have historically subordinated the role of women to those of men, which suggests that socialism is not intrinsically gender-neutral. The book therefore argues that alternatives to capitalism do not represent utopias in any recognized sense; they are not end-points to be realized but processes that must be continually made, reflected upon and remade, if we are to avoid reproducing particular structures of oppression found in old forms of social organization in our alternatives, and if new forms of social organization are not to degenerate into those that came before them.

The social constitution of state, economy and society means that creating an alternative to capitalism on this basis is possible, but it raises an all-important question; how do we go about creating this alternative to capitalism and guard against degeneration back into capitalism and the reproduction of capitalist injustice? This is the question addressed by Chapter 4. In contemporary societies, it is often thought that the democratic process is the most legitimate and appropriate means to pursue our social and economic objectives. However, given that throughout the world there has been a long history of governments led by putatively socialist parties, it is necessary to ask why we have not seen greater moves towards an alternative to capitalism through the democratic process and the institutions of the state; if we have had 'socialist' governments, why have we not had socialism?

Chapter 4 argues that the key reason that we have not seen socialism is because the state is *a capitalist state*. That is to say, the state is a form of prevailing social relationships, and because the prevailing form of social relationships is capitalist, the state reflects the imperatives of that system regardless of the political orientation of the parties in power. It therefore argues that the creation of an alternative to capitalism requires a challenge to the prevailing form of social relations, which includes a challenge to the authority of the state itself. This is not a call to seize state power; history demonstrates too clearly that revolutionary action of this kind quickly descends into despotism and dictatorship as a supposedly 'enlightened' leadership suppress the views of an 'unenlightened mass' in the name of 'the general good'. Rather, it is a call, to use John Holloway's (2005) phrase, to 'change the world without taking power'. This must stem from pluralist and bottom-up social action that is willing to engage with economic and social experimentation.

On the surface, achieving a meaningful change in the world in this way might seem like an impossible task. However, these forms of experimentation have existed for many years, for instance in the cooperative movement and the Zapatista movement, and new forms are emerging with the creation of new commons – for instance, on the internet. Alternatives have in the past, currently are, and in the future can, continue to encroach on capitalist space and create a world that is different to the one with which we are so familiar, and by which we are so frustrated. We are frequently told there is no alternative. Yet the world is what we make of it, which means there is not *an* alternative to capitalism. There are many. All we need to do is make them.

1 | FOUR FACES OF CAPITALISM

Introduction

It is widely accepted that the world we live in is capitalist, and although capitalism may only be lurking in the background as we go about our day-to-day lives, it is nonetheless ever-present as we depend on it as an organizing system to meet our daily needs. It is capitalism which produces food, clothes, housing, energy, and so on. It is also the capitalist system which generally provides (or denies) people the income with which they are able to purchase the things that they need to survive. However, while we know that capitalism is there, the way in which capitalism is understood is not uncontested, and this is an issue of fundamental importance for the decisions we make about whether it is a desirable system. This is important because while capitalism is an organizing system that conditions and shapes our everyday lives, it does not exist outside of us – the people whose very lives it shapes. In this sense, capitalism is constantly being remade or resisted in every social, political and economic transaction that people are involved with. This can be a source of hope, because it means that decisions about the kind of world in which we live are ours to make. However, if we do not ask whether the world in which we live is *the best* world in which we *could* live, it can also be a source of despair; by failing to ask questions about the nature of capitalism, we fail to ask whether the outcomes it produces are fair or just, and our opportunity to address these issues is missed.

Asking questions of the capitalist system is not about criticism of people going about their lives in the capitalist system. As the Marxist philosopher G. A. Cohen (2000: 3) reflected, he 'was taught, as a child, to concentrate [his] judgement on the unjust structure of society, and away from the individuals who happen to benefit from that injustice'. This book argues that such a non-judgemental position is a sensible one to take; people cannot be considered bad people simply for living their lives according to what they perceive to be the prevailing 'rules of the game'. However, if we do not ask questions about those rules and their implications, we cede control over how we remake or resist them, and it is the purpose of this chapter to demonstrate the importance of asking questions about the capitalist system for making decisions about how we organize economy and society.

This chapter asks three specific questions about the rules of the game in order to come to a judgement about the implications of capitalism, and all of them are related to wealth, its *sine qua non*. First, it asks, what is the origin of wealth in a capitalist economy? Secondly, what significance is given to the creation of wealth in a capitalist economy? Finally, what are the implications of how wealth is created and the significance it is given for the role of the state in managing our society? This chapter examines the views of four highly significant political economists on these questions – Adam Smith, Karl Marx, John Maynard Keynes and Friedrich Hayek. Smith is regarded as one of the founding fathers of political economy and (interpretations of) his ideas have played a significant role in the promotion of free markets in the nineteenth and early twentieth centuries, while Marx's work represents a direct criticism of Smith and an enduring and powerful critique of capitalism itself. The views of Keynes and his contemporary Hayek have had a similarly signifi-cant impact on contemporary society, with the former's views heavily shaping the ideas of policy-makers in the period from 1945 to the mid-1970s, and the views of the latter being similarly influential in the period since. The chapter therefore shows how their differing approaches to these questions have profound implications for the form that they believe social, political and economic organization should take. For instance, it shows how Smith's conception of the creation of wealth presents a view of equality in exchange between equals, whereas Marx viewed it as fundamentally reliant on the exploitation of some people by others. It also shows how Keynes believed that the state could intervene in the economy to facilitate the creation of wealth and prosperity, whereas Hayek believed that only the market could achieve these outcomes. In other words, it shows how our ideas about how society *is* organized fundamentally inform our views about whether it *should* be organized differently.

The political economy of Adam Smith

Adam Smith was born in 1723 and was one of the foremost intellectuals of the Scottish Enlightenment. The social, political and economic changes occurring at this time were those that saw social and economic organization begin to take the capitalist form that we recognize today, and Adam Smith was the first to systematically examine it. As Robert Heilbroner (2000: 26–7) has noted, 'Markets have existed as far back as history goes [...] But markets, whether they be exchanges between primitive tribes [...] or the exciting travelling fairs of the Middle Ages, are not the same as the market system.' The market system that emerged in the late seventeenth and early eighteenth centuries was '*a mechanism for sustaining and maintaining an entire society*' (ibid.: 27, emphasis in original).

Prior to the formation of markets as organizing systems, states placed a great deal of emphasis on the acquisition of power and wealth, which was seen to rest in reserves of precious metals. Such a system, known as mercantilism, was founded on two core principles. First, precious metals would always provide the state with 'a financial reserve on hand in liquid form immediately in case of an emergency' (Viner 1930: 270), and, second, 'the only, or the most practicable form in which wealth could be accumulated was in an increase in the national stock of precious metals' (ibid.: 274). In terms of state policy, this led to the prioritization of exports over imports because this was the only way that 'a country with no gold or silver mines' could 'increase its stock of precious metals' (ibid.: 255).

This economic doctrine was intrinsically tied to the maximization of power, as the motivation for the acquisition of wealth in the form of precious metals was 'considered as essential in order to procure [...] desired goods, notably weapons' (Fontanel et al. 2008: 332). Because mercantilists viewed the stock of the world's precious metals to be fixed, the gain of one nation could only come at the expense of other nations, which logically led to adversarial economic competition between states as they sought to secure overseas markets and resources through the exercise of military force (ibid.: 333). The practice was typified by the transfer of gold from South America to Spain and Portugal during the fifteenth century, a practice that was encouraged by policies that 'prohibited the exchange of gold, silver, or [bullion] at a different price than the official parity, and bans on exports [which] forbade the exportation of gold or silver without a license' (Nogues-Marco 2011: 2). Before the middle of the eighteenth century, precious metals were treated as immutable stores of value and wealth, despite the fact that the debasement of precious metals had been used as a means of increasing revenue for the British state by Henry VIII (see Challis 1967) and again in response to the need to pay troops during the Nine Years' War between France and the European Grand Alliance in the 1690s (see Larkin 2006). Mercantilists could not see that the monetary value of bullion was neither finite nor immutable, and as such could not see that it could not be the sole source or manifestation of wealth.

Adam Smith, in contrast, was able to see that equating wealth with the stock of precious metals was a misnomer. In *The Wealth of Nations*, Smith (1776: 293) agreed that 'When [money] is obtained, there is no difficulty in making any subsequent purchase.' However, this was not enough to satisfy him that money was an important end in itself, because precious metals could be 'bought for a certain price like all other commodities' (ibid.: 297–8), and it was plain to Smith that if 'gold and silver should at any time fall short in a country which has wherewithal to purchase them, there are more expedients for supplying their place, than that of almost any other commodity' (ibid.: 299). In other words, precious metals could be purchased with manufactures and natural produce, which could equally be used in order to pay the wages of an army if such a course of action was necessary if a country found itself with a shortage of gold (ibid.: 302). Wealth, then, must be manifest in some other form.

This is the question Smith tackles head-on in Book I of *The Wealth of Nations*. 'The annual labour of every nation', Smith asserts, 'is the fund which originally supplies it with all the necessaries and conveniences of life which it annually consumes' (ibid.: loc. 1). Smith then demonstrates how productive capacity, and therefore wealth, is increased many times through the division of labour because specialization allows people to increase their expertise and skills in a given field, saves time because workers do not have to change tools or places of work between tasks, and encourages the introduction of labour-saving machinery (ibid.: 3). Smith's understanding of the origin of the division of labour is naturalistic, as he argues that it is ingrained in people to 'truck, barter, and exchange one thing for another' (ibid.: 6). For Smith, this natural proclivity to exchange things with others stems from people's self-interest: 'It is not from the benevolence of the butcher, the brewer, or the baker that we expect our dinner, but from their regard to their own interest' (ibid.: 7).

Money and the precious metals that were so important to the early mercantilists are understood by Smith as nothing more than a reflection of value created by production, which facilitates trade by solving problems associated with the coincidence of wants and the indivisibility of commodities. Money is able to efficiently mediate the exchange relationships required by a market economy, but the value in exchange of a commodity is measured by 'the toil and trouble of acquiring it' (ibid.: 19). In primitive economies, in which people carry out many tasks to provide themselves with the necessities of life, the whole value of the produce belongs to the labourer. However, in more advanced economies benefiting from the division of labour, people are reliant on one another in order to be able to create the commodities that can be traded to meet their needs. Workers need the contributions of entrepreneurs who invest in the buildings and machinery that are required to make things, who, in turn, are reliant on landowners for the physical space on which production facilities can be built. As such, in addition to the wages earned by labourers, value must reflect the contributions that stock and land make to production, and so include profits and rents: Smith (ibid.: 32) asserts that once a system of private property has developed, 'the price of every commodity finally resolves itself into some one or other, or all of those three parts; and in every improved society, all the three enter, more or less, as component parts, into the price of the far greater part of commodities'.

Smith therefore argues that the price of a good produced in a market economy benefiting from the division of labour reflects the contributions of all those who have played a part in its production *in proportion* to the contribution they have made.

Adam Smith's understanding of wealth therefore has a number of distinguishing features. First, he was able to see that wealth does not lie in the stock of precious metals, but in the productive capacity of the nation, which is enhanced through the division of labour. Secondly, he believed that this stems from a natural proclivity among people to exchange things with one another and which therefore shows trade to be an, a priori, desirable state of affairs. Thirdly, Smith shows how money represents only the nominal value of a good, while the true value is found in the labour entailed in production. Finally, Smith argues that while the whole value of a product might belong to a labourer in a primitive economy, in a market economy with a division of labour, some of this value must be shared with entrepreneurs and landowners because investment in stock and land also contribute to the production of wealth.

These observations of early market capitalism were pioneering, and justify Adam Smith's reputation as the founding father of political economy analysis. However, it is important to analyse not only Smith's observations about how a market economy operated under the division of labour, but also their implications. One of the most significant implications concerns Smith's belief that the propensity for people to barter and exchange goods was something in their nature. Smith thought desirable outcomes would be reached through such exchanges, motivated by self-interest rather than benevolence, even though a person 'neither intends to promote the public interest, nor knows how much he is promoting it'; rather, people are 'led by an invisible hand to promote an end which was no part of [their] intention' (ibid.: 313). In social terms, Smith believed that a person 'frequently promotes [the interest] of society more effectually than when [they] really [intend] to promote it' (ibid.: 313).

Given Smith's emphasis on self-interest, it is clear to see how his work might be used in order to justify a state of affairs in which every individual should act selfishly, because this will promote the general good. This argument is politically conservative because it could be used in order to oppose any redistribution of incomes and wealth on the basis that such actions would distort the optimum outcomes Smith believed would arise by virtue of the interaction between self-interested action and the invisible hand. However, such a reading of Smith fails to appreciate his status not only as one of the eighteenth century's pre-eminent political economists, but also as one of the eighteenth century's pre-eminent moral philosophers.

Matthew Watson (2005) helpfully illustrates this point. He notes that while Smith talks of 'self-interest', the kind of actors that he describes are not 'selfish'; his agents have socially based moral principles that stem from people's ability to sympathize with one another (ibid.: 114). While Smith's theory of existence remains individual and liberal, his conception of 'self-interest' includes a concern for the social whole as people's consciences are *learned* through interaction with others (ibid.: 117), and come to reflect a desire to treat others as one would wish to be treated. In a later contribution, Watson (2012: 463) has described Smith's approach to sympathy as 'a plausible philosophical mechanism to explain why people would cede the right to distribute their property in whatever way they deemed best in order to privilege the competing claims of the nation's development profile' – to encourage the wealth of the nation.

A second area in which it is necessary to consider the implications of Smith's work relates to the way in which he sees the division of labour as the *cause* and not an *effect* of increases in the proficiency of people to produce goods and provide services in a market economy. 'The difference of natural talents in different men', Smith (1776: 8) wrote, 'is, in reality, much less than we are aware of', and the differences in ability that it is possible to identify between people in a market economy are understood 'not upon many occasions so much the cause, as the effect of the division of labour' (ibid.: 8). In arguing that the difference between a philosopher and a street porter 'seems to arise not so much from nature, as from habit' (ibid.: 8), Smith puts forward an argument that strikes a chord with the founding principles of the United States and the opening lines of the *Declaration of Independence*, published in the same year as Smith's *The Wealth of Nations*, that it is a 'self-evident truth' that 'all men are created equal'.

The implications of such an argument, once again, are politically conservative; if all people are born the same then it is possible to make a case against political involvement in the creation of equality of opportunity, since this occurs naturally. On the basis of the claim to interpersonal equivalence, the absence of redistribution of incomes and wealth can be justified because all social outcomes are the products only of individual choices. Everybody, under such circumstances, benefits from the division of labour, because it is the division of labour which allows people to enhance their skills and increase their own personal well-being, as well as the well-being of the social group more broadly.

In reality, it is clearly the case that not all people are created equal, and inherent physical and mental differences between them, as well as socially constructed differences such as class, race and gender, play a significant role in shaping the particular place occupied by different people in social and economic hierarchies. This fails to recognize the distinction between option luck – matters of 'how deliberate and calculated gambles turn out' – and brute luck – matters of 'how risks fall out that are not in that sense deliberate gambles' (Dworkin 1981: 293), and it is the fact that people clearly are not created equal which has led theorists of social justice such as John Rawls (1985: 236) to argue that it is necessary for us to make judgements about a just distribution of resources from behind 'a veil of ignorance'. He argues that we must abstract from 'the contingencies of the social world' in a way that allows us to 'eliminate the bargaining advantages which inevitably arise within background institutions of any society as the result of cumulative social, historical and natural tendencies'. However, Smith's notion that differences between people are principally derived naturally from the division of labour and the individual choices – which are made freely from equal starting positions – that shape the division of labour, provides a clear rationale against redistribution in the context of a market system that is understood to promote the general interest through people's self-interested actions.

A third area in which it is possible to critique Adam Smith's political economy relates to his conception of value, and specifically the way in which he perceives prices to be a reflection of the contributions of stock, land and labour to production. Insofar as all contributors to production are understood to receive the value of their contribution to production, this does not appear intrinsically problematic. As Simon Clarke (2011 [1982]: loc. 550) notes, because 'profit, rent and wages were independent component parts of the value of a commodity [...] there was no reason to conclude that increasing rents and profits were at the expense of wages'. However, in something of a paradox, it was Smith's argument that rising wages and rents would not result in falls in profits but lead to increases in prices that would be passed on to consumers. In the process, the distinction between producers and consumers failed 'to recognize that the consumer could ultimately only be the wage-labourer, capitalist or land-owner wearing another hat' (ibid.: loc. 550), which in turn meant any nominal increase they received in wages, profits or rent would be eroded in real terms by the increase in price. In other words, the possibility of wage labourers increasing their relative wealth by improving their conditions of employment was limited by the fact that the increase in the cost of production that it caused would be passed on to them in the form of higher prices.

This notion of equality in exchange in the process of wealth creation can once again be interpreted in a politically conservative way. This is because although Smith believed that a wide franchise was desirable to 'ensure that as many people as possible are able to defend their rights' (Clarke 2011 [1988]: loc. 1369–86), he also thought that 'The ignorance of the poor prevents them from appreciating the benefits that accrue to them from the security of property and the freedom of exchange' (ibid.: loc. 950–64). On the one hand, this justified the public provision of education (ibid.: loc. 1013; Clarke 2011 [1982]: loc. 650; West 1969: 10), but also raised fears about the tyranny of the majority, which Smith thought might rise to attack private property because it failed to recognize the benefits he believed were derived from it;

> Since the theory of political economy established that the working class had no distinct interest, it had no particular need of independent political representation. By the same token women had no need of independent representation since their interests were adequately represented by their fathers and husbands. (Clarke 2011 [1988]: loc. 1377–92)

On the basis of Smith's belief in the equality of exchange, derived from his theory of value in a developed economy under the division of labour, it was therefore possible to make a case for excluding large elements of the population from the political process in a way that is anathema to contemporary understandings of liberal democracy. Nonetheless, Smith's failure to identify the origin of profits and rent as a deduction from the value produced by labour does not mean that he was unable to recognize pernicious aspects of the division of labour. For instance, Smith did recognize that although the division of labour promotes the dexterity of people with regard to certain skills, these are very limited and may result in the curtailment of people's intellect, which in some respects pre-empts the Marxist concept of alienation. However, as E. G. West (1969: 7) noted, Smith did not fully appreciate the powerlessness or isolation at the heart of the concept of alienation developed by later political economists because he saw the division of labour as the 'means of man's economic "liberation" from nature's niggardly environment' and as working 'towards, not against the direction of social intercourse' by bringing production together (ibid.: 10). As such, Smith's notion that people will not fulfil their potential without the division of labour and will have their potential stifled within the division of labour is an uneasy one (ibid.: 11).

While Adam Smith's political economy is often associated with the 'free' market, and things like his naturalistic conception of the division of labour, the invisible hand and the constituent component of price theory of value seem to emphasize the importance of the market *over* the state, it is important to note that Smith believed the state was absolutely essential for the operation of capitalism. In his words, political economy should be viewed 'as a branch of the science of a statesman or legislator' (Smith 1776: 292). In conditions where there was no state, it would not be possible for the various kinds of action necessary to coordinate the division of labour, such as the protection of private property, to take place. The state is therefore necessary to create and preserve the conditions in which the division of labour can develop on the basis of trade between people. Provisions for the protection of private property and national defence are therefore important features of Adam Smith's state; however, while the state must be strong in order to achieve these aims, its role is strictly limited to creating the conditions in which the market can operate most efficiently; because Smith believed that the division of labour would occur naturally from people acting in their self-interest in the marketplace, and because he believed that this would benefit all people in society (whether they realized it or not), no further extension of state competencies was necessary or justified.

Karl Marx's critique of political economy

Adam Smith's work in political economy was pioneering, but not uncontroversial. This is because his views on the development of the division of labour, the role of self-interest and his theory of value can be used to promote politically conservative positions (even if these positions sometimes go beyond Smith's intentions when considered in the context of his moral philosophy). However, Smith did believe that the creation of wealth through the division of labour is *inherently* desirable, and that the state should play a role in ensuring that the benefits of this can be achieved. It is here that the political economy of Karl Marx differs from that of Adam Smith. While Marx was able to see that the division of labour produced wealth, and that the state played an important role in creating conditions for this to happen, his analysis showed that the creation of wealth did not produce benefits for all classes distributed according to their contribution to the creation of value, but was reliant on the exploitation of one class by another. It is in this respect that Marx's work is a *critique of political economy*.

As capitalist wealth is comprised of the stock of commodities, Marx develops his critique of political economy in *Capital*, volume I, with an analysis of commodities. He notes how all commodities have a use-value – a usefulness to people in terms of the utility provided – and an exchange value – what a given commodity is worth in terms of other commodities (which may or may not be money) (Marx 1990 [1867]: 126). Observing the simple barter economy, Marx (ibid.: 127) notes how all commodities can be exchanged for given quantities of many different kinds of commodities: 'a quarter of wheat for example, is exchanged for x boot-polish, y silk or z gold, etc.'. Each commodity therefore has a single use-value but many exchange values. It is logically derived from this observation that the relation between two commodities expressed in terms of their exchange values shows that 'a common element of identical magnitude exists in two different things [...] Both are therefore equal to a third thing, which in itself is neither the one nor the other. Each of them, so far as it is exchange-value, must therefore be reducible to this third thing' (ibid.: 127).

In other words, as all commodities can be exchanged for given quantities of all other commodities, they must have something in common. Marx (ibid.: 128) proposes that this property in common cannot be something natural, because natural properties pertain to the usefulness of a commodity and not its value in exchange. As such, 'If then we disregard the use-value of commodities, only one property remains, that of being products of labour' (ibid.: 128).

It is in the fact that commodities are the products of human labour that their value – 'the common factor in the exchange relation' (ibid.: 128) – lies. Here, Marx observes an oddity in the sense that 'It might seem that if the value of a commodity is determined by the quantity of labour expended to produce it, it would be the more valuable the more unskilful and lazy the worker who produced it, because he would take more time to complete the article' (ibid.: 129). However, Marx insists value exists in *socially necessary* labour time, which 'is the labour-time required to produce any use-value under the conditions of production normal for a given society and with the average degree of skill and intensity of labour prevalent in that society' (ibid.: 129). Through the act of exchange, mediated by money, production allows for the use-values of commodities to be realized.

However, under capitalism, Marx argues that commodities are not produced for their use-value itself, but for their exchange values; capitalism is distinguished from other forms of social organization by its intention to turn money into more money, and Marx therefore defines *capital* as value in motion. This process begins with capitalists' acquisition of two kinds of commodities. The first is the means of production, which refers to raw materials, buildings, machinery, and so on. The second is labour-power, which is the commoditized form of labour. That is to say, the concept of labour-power distinguishes 'workers themselves from their ability or capacity to work' (Fine and Saad-Filho 2010: 20). The intention of the capitalist is to combine these commodities in the production process so that the sum realized in exchange of the commodities produced exceeds the sum outlaid on the acquisition of the means of production and labour-power. The problem, as Marx (1990 [1867]: 268–9) conceived it, is how money is transformed into capital from a starting point that involves 'the exchange of equivalents'. As Ben Fine and Alfredo Saad-Filho (2010: 32) have phrased it, for this to occur, 'among the commodities purchased by the capitalist there must be one or more that creates more value than it costs'.

As Marx had previously established that it is labour and labour alone which creates value, it cannot be the means of production which *adds* value, because it can only contribute value 'as a result of the labour time socially necessary to produce them in the past [...] for otherwise money would be growing magically on trees, or at least, in machines' (ibid.: 32). As such, the ability of capitalists to turn money into more money lies in their ability to extract more value from labour than they pay for it. This can be achieved because there is a difference between the exchange value and the use-value of labour-power. To demonstrate it, Marx makes the assumption that the socially necessary labour time to re-create labour-power (its value) is 3 shillings, or half a day's labour. The capitalist pays 3 shillings for the value of labour-power (its exchange value) and the labourer adds value to the production of new commodities. An exchange of equivalent values takes place. However, 'The fact that half a day's labour is necessary to keep the worker alive during 24 hours does not in any way prevent him from working a whole day' (Marx 1990 [1867]: 300). The use-value of labour-power to the capitalist therefore exceeds the amount the capitalist pays for it, and the difference between the two is appropriated by the capitalist as surplus value. Marx (ibid.: 301) summarizes the process like this:

> On the one hand the daily sustenance of labour-power costs
> only half a day's labour, while on the other hand the very same
> labour-power can remain effective, can work, during a whole day,
> and consequently the value which its use during one day creates is
> double what the capitalist pays for that use. (Ibid.: 301)

Under capitalist production, then, wealth can be accumulated because the wage labourer parts with the use-value of their labour-power for its lower exchange value, and the difference between the two is appropriated by the capitalist as surplus value which constitutes their profit.

Marx (ibid.: 301) notes how 'this circumstance is a piece of good luck for the buyer [of labour-power], but by no means an injustice towards the seller'. This is true in the sense that the labourer receives the value of their labour-power in exchange for their work. However, Marx also describes the way in which the process allows for money's transformation into capital, as value creates more value, as 'a trick' (ibid.: 301). This suggests that the appearance of equality in exchange is simply a charade in which money conceals the distinction between use-values and exchange values and allows for the appropriation of value by one class of people from another on an apparently equal footing. The foundations on which this 'trick' rely are very particular:

> For the transformation of money into capital [...] the owner of money must find the free worker available on the commodity-market; and this worker must be free in the double sense that as a free individual he can dispose of his labour-power as his own commodity, and that, on the other hand, he has no other commodity for sale, i.e. he is rid of them, he is free of all of the objects needed for the realization of his labour power. (Ibid.: 273)

The accumulation of wealth in capitalism is therefore dependent on the 'double freedom' of the labourer. However, the nature of this double freedom poses an interesting question: If a worker is 'free' in the sense that they are not a slave, but has no option but to sell their labour-power to the market in a system that exploits the difference between its value and the value it can create, what is the nature of this 'freedom', beyond the freedom to starve? Is the worker really free at all?

G. A. Cohen (1982: 3) points out that some people would argue that a 'free' worker in the Marxist sense does not have to sell their labour-power because they can choose to rely on welfare or charity, or their luck. He also notes that people are free to starve in the sense that nobody will force a person to stay alive. However, he rejects this notion of what it is to be free by arguing that a person is forced to do something when they are left with 'no *reasonable* or *acceptable* alternative course' (ibid.: 4, emphasis in original). While it may well be the case that routes out of the proletariat exist, for instance by securing positions in the petty bourgeoisie through long hours and hard work, which make it difficult to claim workers are 'forced' to sell their labour-power (ibid.: 7), the choices to rely on charity or luck, or to starve, cannot be considered reasonable or acceptable. Therefore, it is possible to see that when Marx discusses the 'freedom' of workers to sell the one commodity they own, he does so with a certain sense of irony.

In his conception of wealth, Marx therefore identifies an intrinsic and inherent contradiction between two classes – the proletariat that has nothing to sell but their labour-power, and the bourgeoisie that owns the means of production. As labour alone creates value, and capitalism is a system that seeks to realize profit, it is also a system that is dependent on the exploitation of one class of people by another, as workers are paid less for their labour-power than the value it creates. It is also fundamentally dependent on the initial separation of this class of people from the means of subsistence. Without the proletarianized worker, who has no way to meet their everyday needs other than through the sale of their labour-power, it would not be possible for capitalism to exist. In other words, Marx's conception of the way in which wealth is created in capitalism suggests that the system is fundamentally dependent on the impoverishment of large sections of the population. Moreover, the process is not a static one; it is not the case that proletarianized workers are exploited through their separation from the means of subsistence and subjected to wage labour once and for all. Under capitalism, the process of their impoverishment and subjugation is ongoing and increasingly antagonistic.

This is because competition between capitalist firms leads them to seek a competitive advantage over one another, and two primary ways in which this can be achieved are through lowering the wages paid for the purchase of labour-power, and increasing the productivity of industry by replacing labour with machinery. The first has obvious implications for wage rates, and the second has implications for unemployment, which serves to reinforce downward pressure on wages even further. The logic of capitalist competition, therefore, is dependent on the 'impoverishment' and 'deskilling' of workers, which 'exacerbates class struggle' (Clarke 2001: 96–8). The book will return to this point in its discussion of inherent crisis tendencies in capitalism in the next chapter.

As capital is dependent on the exploitation of labour for its existence, it is possible to derive very different judgements about the role of the state to those reached by Adam Smith. While Smith acknowledged that the state was necessary in order to create conditions for the operation of the market, the state was perceived as a facilitator of the capitalist market system that would allow benefits to be realized by all of society. Marx, on the other hand, agreed that the state is necessary for capital to exist, but was able to see that this function was far from beneficial for all members of society. In sustaining the system of private property through the enforcement of contracts, he suggests that the state persistently plays a role in maintaining the separation of workers from their means of subsistence. In managing the national currency as the means of exchange of private property (including labour-power), the state also serves to create and consolidate the appearance of equality in exchange relations that are profoundly unequal. In effect, the state facilitates the means by which labourers are continually subjected to the discipline of starvation so that capitalists can continue to exploit the difference between the amount workers are paid and the value they create. As such, Marx and Engels (1985 [1848]: 82) suggested that the 'executive of the modern state' is nothing 'but a committee for managing the common affairs of the whole bourgeoisie'.

Keynesian political economy

The previous two sections have shown how both Adam Smith and Karl Marx believed that the accumulation of wealth was dependent on the production of commodities. However, whereas Smith believed this was a naturalistic process that benefited everyone in proportion to their contribution to the wealth created, Marx's analysis showed how the process was dependent on the exploitation of one class by another. While both agreed that the state was necessary for capitalism to operate, Smith believed its role was to create conditions that allowed everybody to realize the benefits of the division of labour, while Marx believed the role of the state was to create and re-create conditions under which workers were separated from their means of subsistence, and forced to sell their labour-power on the market to be exploited for a profit. This section considers John Maynard Keynes' analysis of how wealth is maximized through its movement through the economy, and how this can be encouraged by the state.

Before Keynes was writing in the 1920s and 1930s, the focus of political economy analysis had begun to shift. In a period known as the *methodenstreit* – the debate over methods – the political economy tradition of producing a scientific understanding of how the economy works in the abstract, which was combined with a consideration of the practical and normative implications of the economy's operation, was increasingly abandoned (see Gamble 1995; Watson 2005). Economics emerged as a distinct discipline from political economy, and as Andrew Gamble (1995: 518) noted, economics 'directed attention away from analysing the social basis of capitalism towards analysing how choices are made between alternative ends under conditions of scarcity'. This resulted in a view of economics on the one hand as a science, and on the other as a discipline that could tell only half-truths about artificial scenarios, and which is often referred to as neoclassical economics. Mark Blaug (1997: 282) has stated that 'an unkind critic might say that neoclassical economics indeed achieved greater generality but only by asking easier questions'. Others have gone farther. Thomas Rice (1993: 201), for instance, has quipped that if an economist were stranded on a desert island with nothing other than canned food and no can opener, their solution to their impending starvation would be to 'Assume we have a can opener.'

John Maynard Keynes was a twentieth-century political economist who resisted these tendencies, and returned to the traditions of Smith and Marx. Having studied under one of the leading neoclassical economists, Alfred Marshall, Keynes was familiar with economic analysis but frustrated by its assertion that over the long run markets would tend towards equilibrium. As he stated it: 'This *long-run* is a misleading guide to current affairs. *In the long run we are all dead.* Economists set themselves too easy, too useless a task if in tempestuous seasons they can only tell us that when the storm is past the ocean is flat again' (Keynes 1924: 110, emphasis in original).

The key question about how we make the most efficient use of resources in a capitalist economy must therefore be supplemented by another important consideration. The 'outstanding characteristic of the economic system in which we live', Keynes wrote, is that 'whilst it is subject to severe fluctuations in respect of output and employment [...] it seems capable of remaining in a chronic condition of subnormal activity for a considerable period without any marked tendency either towards recovery or towards complete collapse' (Keynes 2008 [1936]: 158–9). Keynes therefore asked why, under certain conditions, the process through which wealth was created stalled, and what the state could do in order to prevent this from happening.

Keynes did not embark on a systematic analysis of commodity production in order to establish the origins of wealth as Smith and Marx before him had done. By the time that Keynes was writing, this fact was taken for granted. However, Keynes was concerned with how wealth expanded in the economy, and he therefore focused on the way that money's circulation throughout the economy created wealth. This began from the simple observation that every person's income is dependent on another person's expenditure, and the logically derived position that maintaining levels of expenditure is of fundamental importance for maintaining (and increasing) levels of income. As Robert Heilbroner (2000: 265) has phrased it, 'It is by this process of handing money around – taking in each other's wash, it has been described – that the economy is constantly revitalized.' Keynes also noted that this process has the potential to be self-reinforcing because when expenditure provides jobs and incomes, these incomes create possibility for new expenditures that can create new jobs and new incomes, and so on. This potential for an initial investment to have an exponential effect on the national income is known as the multiplier effect.

On the basis of these observations, Keynes (2008 [1936]: 22–3) viewed the national income as the sum of the aggregate income that is generated by the prevailing level of employment in the economy. Given that the national income is maximized if every person individually has a high income, it naturally follows that it is desirable for the level of employment to be kept high. 'The amount of employment, both in each individual firm and industry and the aggregate', Keynes argued, 'depends on the amount of the proceeds which the entrepreneurs expect to receive from the corresponding output.' In other words, firms and industries will employ one extra worker so long as the value that the extra worker is expected to create exceeds its cost. This is because it is rational for entrepreneurs 'to fix the amount of employment at the level which they expect to maximize the excess of the proceeds over the factor costs' (ibid.: 23). For Keynes (ibid.: 25, emphasis in original),

> The amount of labor N which the entrepreneurs decide to employ depends on the sum (D) of two quantities [...] the amount which the community is expected to spend on consumption, and [...] the amount which it is expected to devote to new investment. D is what we have called [...] the *effective demand*.

This means that the level of employment will be dependent on the expectations of capitalists about the profits that can be made from any given level of employment, and on the basis that the ability of entrepreneurs to make a return on their investments depends on the existence of a market for their products and services, a fully employed waged economy seems to be desirable, a priori. It is in the context of these observations about how wealth expands in the economy that Keynes addressed the problem of how capitalism can remain in a prolonged period of depression.

As employment is a product of expenditure (because firms hire workers when they expect to sell goods of a greater value), and because expenditure is, by definition, the sum of consumption and investment, for full employment and a high national income to be secured, it is necessary to ensure that consumption and investment remain high. Keynes asks why this isn't the case, and observes that if money were used only as a medium of exchange, there would be no problem because all incomes would be subsequently used as expenditure or investment, creating a virtuous cycle through the operation of the multiplier effect. However, because money is also used as a store of value, there are three specific ways in which money can be lost from the 'circular flow of incomes' that generates wealth, which have a corresponding impact on the level of economic activity, and therefore employment. These are household savings, government taxation of households and firms, and expenditure on exports, because each represents a withdrawal of money from the economy to use it as a store of value rather than as a medium of exchange. However, none of these leakages from the circular flow of income is inherently problematic because each has a counterparty to offset the leakage: household savings in financial institutions can be loaned for the purposes of business investment or consumption; taxation can be offset by government expenditure; and expenditure on imports can be offset by revenue from exports. Therefore, as long as investment is equal to savings, government expenditure equals government revenue, and the balance of payments is in equilibrium or surplus (exports are equal to or greater than imports), then the circular flow of income will continue uninterrupted and the economy will not find itself in recession or depression (see Stilwell 2012: 273–5).

The national income (or the wealth of a nation) can therefore be defined as the sum of consumption, investment, government expenditure and exports, minus that spent on imports, and 'If these components are growing (shrinking in the case of [imports]), then the national income will tend to grow' (ibid.: 277). In theory, then, the movement of wealth throughout the economy could be unproblematic, and indeed a virtuous cycle of growth might even be established. In practice, however, this does not occur because money is not always recirculated into the economy because of the way in which individuals' and households' propensity to consume and firms' propensity to invest are affected by uncertainty in the economy.

There are a number of factors that affect a person's propensity to consume goods. These include the level of wages, the level of income minus taxation (and, therefore, fiscal policy), changes in the value of capital goods such as housing, and changes in the purchasing power of money (inflation/deflation) (Keynes 2008 [1936]: 62–4). While the propensity to consume expressed in terms of these objective factors appears to be stable in the sense that aggregate consumption is dependent on aggregate income, Keynes introduces a 'fundamental psychological law, upon which we are entitled to depend with great confidence' from 'our knowledge of human nature' and 'from the detailed facts of experience' (ibid.: 65). This is that people 'are disposed, as a rule and on the average, to increase their consumption as their income increases, but not by as much as the increase in their income' (ibid.: 65). In other words, there is a propensity towards saving in a capitalist economy, which stems at the household level from eight sources. First, to provide a reserve for unforeseen expenditures (precaution); secondly, to provide for a future change in the relationship between income and family needs, for example in old age (foresight); thirdly, to amass interest by deferring current for future expenditure (calculation); fourthly, to provide for a gradual increase in expenditure over time (improvement); fifthly, to secure the power to do things without a specific aim (independence); sixthly, to speculate or engage in entrepreneurial activities (enterprise); seventhly, to leave money after one's death (pride); and, finally, to be miserly (avarice) (see ibid.: 72). Governments and businesses have four corresponding reasons to withhold from consumption. First, to secure resources for further investment (enterprise); secondly, to retain reserves to deal with unforeseen circumstances (liquidity); thirdly, to secure rising income to insulate government or management from criticism (improvement); and, finally, to pay down debt (prudence) (ibid.: 72–3).

As noted above, these leakages from the circular flow of income are not problematic if they are saved in banks and the money is lent onwards for investment, and given the multiplier effect – where any increase in aggregate investment causes a higher increase in aggregate employment because those employed from the first round of investment spend a proportion of their incomes and therefore provide money for investment to other firms and so on – may even be beneficial. However, just as people do not always wish to spend, firms do not always wish to invest, and will only do so if they feel that every extra pound (or dollar or euro, etc.) spent will generate more than the sum invested in revenue (ibid.: 88–95). This is known as the 'marginal efficiency of capital', and is fundamentally dependent on *expectations*, which are a product of forecasts that are made and the degree of confidence that is held in them (ibid.: 96). However, because the future is uncertain and not subject to accurate probability calculations, decisions are dependent on people's intuition:

> [I]ndividual initiative will only be adequate when reasonable calculation is supplemented and supported by animal spirits, so that the thought of ultimate loss which often overtakes pioneers, as experience undoubtedly tells us and them, is put aside as a healthy man puts aside the expectation of death.
> This means, unfortunately, not only that slumps and

depressions are exaggerated in degree, but that economic prosperity is excessively dependent on a political and social atmosphere which is congenial to the average business man. (Ibid.: 105)

Keynes therefore developed a sophisticated understanding of how wealth in the economy was generated and circulated, as well as how this process tended towards disruption. In light of this, clear policy implications can be derived about the ability of the state to move the economy out of depression by using public expenditure to boost employment, which will subsequently have a positive knock-on effect as those newly employed people are able to spend a proportion of their incomes and in the process provide funds for investment by the private sector. However, while Keynes believed that the government should be concerned with the level of unemployment, and act to maintain it, this was not because he was a socialist. Indeed, Keynes (ibid.: 234) explicitly noted that he believed 'there is social and psychological justification for significant inequalities of incomes and wealth' because 'There are valuable human activities which require the motive of money-making and the environment of private wealth-ownership for their full fruition.' In fact, he described his own theory as 'moderately conservative' on the basis that he did not think the state should assume control of the means of production. 'It is not the ownership of the instruments of production', Keynes (ibid.: 236) wrote, 'which it is important for the state to assume. If the state is able to determine the aggregate amount of resources devoted to augmenting the instruments and the basic rate of reward to those who own them, it will have accomplished all that is necessary.'

Keynes' theory is therefore one that is concerned with the well-being of society holistically conceived rather than prioritizing the interests of a certain sector of society. It is here that we can see important normative differences from Marx, because Keynes does not challenge capitalism on the basis of fundamental injustices in the way that wealth is created, but only in terms of how its adjustment mechanisms are insufficient to provide for continued prosperity.

However, it is equally true that Keynes did not believe in the capitalist ethos for its own sake. He thought that the purpose of acquiring wealth was to be able to use it to enjoy one's life. 'Why should anyone outside a lunatic asylum', Keynes (1937: 216) asked, 'wish to use money as a store of wealth?' He believed money should be spent so as to enjoy a good life. This qualification of the purpose of economic activity is extremely significant. As Robert Skidelsky (2010: 131) wrote:

> Keynes was a philosopher and moralist as well as an economist. He never ceased to question the purposes of economic activity. Briefly stated, his conclusion was that the pursuit of money – what he called 'love of money' – was justified only to the extent that it led to a 'good life' [...] To make the world ethically better was the only justifiable purpose of economic striving.

In other words, it was Keynes' belief that we should pursue our endeavours to create wealth until such a point was reached at which each and every member of society was able to live such a good life, and it was the state's role to nurse a system with a tendency towards depression through times of hardship until this was reached.

Moreover, Keynes believed that significant moves towards the good life were being made, and that the depression of the interwar period was simply 'a temporary phase of maladjustment' as societies got used to the labour that was saved by the introduction of machinery into production (Keynes 1930: 3). Unlike Marx, who saw technological innovation as a product of competition that consolidated labourers' separation from the means of subsistence, Keynes saw it as holding the potential to increase people's standard of living – he estimated by a magnitude of between four and eight times between 1930 and 2030 (ibid.: 3). On this basis, and given the absolute nature of certain human needs – those of subsistence – Keynes believed that 'assuming no important wars and no important increase in population, the *economic problem* may be solved, or be at least within sight of solution, within a hundred years' (ibid.: 4, emphasis in original). This did not mean that people would no longer need to work – it would still be necessary to produce goods and people will have a desire to work because it is ingrained in their nature. However, it was his view that 'Three-hour shifts or a fifteen-hour week may put off the problem for a great while. For three hours a day is quite enough to satisfy the old Adam in most of us!' (ibid.: 5).

One of the key contributions of Keynesian political economy was the observation that the income of any one individual is dependent on the income of another individual, which meant that for wealth to expand employment must remain high. If it did, a virtuous cycle could be established as people employed in the one round of investments spend some of their income, which can be used to fund further investment, and so on. Another important observation was the contradiction between money's functions as a medium of exchange and as a store of value, which meant that in times of uncertainty people and firms would save, reducing progressively the expenditures available to be used as incomes for others. As such, Keynes' view of capitalism provided a strong rationale for the intervention of the state to provide investment at times when individual and corporate uncertainty led to saving, because this could provide employment and help re-create the virtuous cycle of wealth creation until the point at which all people could live the 'good life' was reached.

Hayek's free economy and strong state

Friedrich Hayek was born in Vienna on the cusp of the twentieth century, and worked at a number of prestigious academic institutions, including the London School of Economics and Political Science (1931–50) and the University of Chicago (1950–62). Writing during the depression of the interwar period and following the Second World War, Hayek was a contemporary of Keynes, and therefore was also attempting to address the kinds of problems associated with the neoclassical turn in economics – especially its failure to understand how capitalism found itself in prolonged periods of suboptimal output. Nonetheless, in considering how resources could be used most efficiently in order to maximize the creation of wealth for society, Hayek reached significantly different conclusions about the operation of the capitalist economy from Keynes, which had profoundly different implications for what he believed the state should and could do in order to assist in its smooth operation.

The central problem as conceived by Friedrich Hayek was how markets could reach equilibrium in the absence of a central organizing institution or set of institutions that possessed sufficient information to plan for such an outcome, and how wealth could be maximized as a result. As Ronald McKinnon (1992: 31) has noted, Hayek placed a strong emphasis on his belief that markets could *spontaneously* produce economic equilibrium of this kind through market interaction. Hayek therefore believed that the creation and expansion of wealth were dependent on the ability of the market to coordinate itself spontaneously in this way. Hayek (1937) equated equilibrium with a scenario in which the plans of every single actor in a social grouping could be executed without adjustment to take account of the effects of other people's plans. He believed that the plan of every individual was the product of the information that they have available to them and the expectations of future actions that they produce. The ability for an individual to successfully execute their own plan is therefore fundamentally dependent on other members of society having compatible plans. If the plans are not compatible, then the equilibrium will come to an end until other plans are adjusted and they become compatible again. As Hayek (ibid.: 41, emphasis in original) phrased it: 'For a society then we *can* speak of a *state* of equilibrium at a point of time – but it means only that compatibility exists between the different plans which the individuals composing it have made for action in time.' Furthermore, 'this state will continue, once it exists, so long as the external data correspond to the common expectations of all the members of the society' (ibid.: 41).

In order to illustrate his point, Hayek (ibid.: 42–3) asks us to imagine the preparations for a programme of house building, in which brick-makers, plumbers and other tradespeople prepare materials to build a certain number of houses. They are dependent on each other to have the same expectations of the number of houses to be built, as well as the plans of savers to buy houses, if they are to carry out their own plans without having to adjust them. 'This', Hayek (ibid.: 42) notes, 'need not be so, because other circumstances which are not part of their plan of action may turn out to be different from what they expected.' For instance, 'Part of the materials may be destroyed by an accident' (ibid.: 42), which can be referred to as an *objective* disruption in planning. Or, 'if the different plans were from the beginning incompatible, it is inevitable that somebody's plans will be upset and have to be altered' (ibid.: 43), which can be referred to as a *subjective* disruption in planning. Like Keynes, then, Hayek is concerned with the problems for the economy caused by uncertainty, or in his terms, the fragmented nature of knowledge in society, which means that in all likelihood people will have to continually adjust their plans in order to achieve their goals because they are unlikely to be compatible with other people's plans from the outset. If people's plans are compatible, then it will be possible for wealth to be created and expanded efficiently, as markets will find themselves in equilibrium. This raises the question of how people use this fragmented knowledge efficiently in order to produce optimal outcomes for the production and use of wealth in a capitalist economy.

For Hayek (ibid.: 52), the 'spontaneous actions of individuals will [...] bring about a distribution of resources which can be understood as if it were made according to a single plan, although nobody has planned it'. This possibility is realized through the mechanism of competition, which helps people to identify the information that is relevant for them to make their own decisions by acting as a discovery procedure. This places a great deal of emphasis on the knowledge of particular circumstances rather than a holistic or all-encompassing knowledge of economy and society: 'the knowledge of the circumstances of which we must make use never exists in concentrated or integrated form, but solely as the dispersed bits of incomplete and frequently contradictory knowledge which all the separate individuals possess' (Hayek 1945: 519).

Again, Hayek asks us to imagine a hypothetical situation – this time one in which a particular raw material that is used domestically but produced overseas becomes scarce for one reason or another. This could be the result of exhausting the supply of the raw material or because a change in the political circumstances of the country of origin disrupts the supply. In the face of this disruption in supply, something that we can describe as an objective disruption, those manufacturers relying on this particular raw material will find that less is imported into the country. As materials become scarce, the price increases and users of the raw material either need to reduce other costs or, more likely, to find a substitute good that allows them to execute their plans at the same cost. As prices increase when supply becomes scarce the competitive price system filters all of the information that users of this raw material need – namely, that it has become scarce. It does not matter why the supply of this particular raw material has become scarce to its users, because they can respond to signals from the price system in order to make the necessary judgements about the use of substitute goods and adjust their plans accordingly. Therefore, in a world where it is impossible to command all of the information necessary to make rational economic decisions with perfect foresight, as neoclassical economists had assumed, Hayek could nonetheless conceive of the way in which markets might reach equilibrium as *relevant* information is transmitted to interested parties from localities where it is possessed to localities where it is not, through the price system (ibid.: 525–6).

In Hayek's understanding, then, it is the way in which the market operates which allows for diverse and fragmented information to be transmitted to individuals executing their plans, and allows for equilibrium to be reached. It is through this process that economies can operate efficiently and wealth can be created and expanded. He did not think that there is a role for the state to play in encouraging the development of wealth, either through direct intervention in individual firms or industries, or by redistributing wealth from those who possess it to those who do not. Indeed, Hayek (2001 [1945]: 31) casts the role of the state in the worst possible light. First, he establishes links between historical tendencies towards planning in Germany and trends in America and England, which he describes as 'the increasing veneration for the state, the fatalistic acceptance of "inevitable trends", the enthusiasm for "organization" of everything'. Then, more dramatically and devastatingly for advocates of planning, he goes on to establish links between this planning and the Nazi regime of Adolf Hitler:

> The supreme tragedy is still not seen that in Germany it was largely people of good will who, by their socialist policies, prepared the way for the forces which stand for everything they detest. Few recognize that the rise of fascism and Marxism was not a reaction against the socialist trends of the preceding period *but a necessary outcome of those tendencies*. (Ibid.: 31–2, emphasis in original)

In other words, it was not because people were intrinsically affiliated with or sympathetic towards the ethos of the Nazis, but because tendencies towards socialism had led to a reliance on the state, that the rise of such fascist regimes was not only possible but also inevitable. '[I]t is significant', Hayek (ibid.: 32) wrote, 'that many of the leaders of these movements, from Mussolini down [...], began as socialists and ended as fascists or Nazis.'

Andrew Gamble (1996a: 47) has neatly summarized Hayek's position on the relationship between planning and the rise of dictatorial regimes, noting that Hayek believed 'there existed no middle way between capitalism and socialism, with even the mildest measures of state intervention capable of pushing a society towards totalitarianism'. In order to produce conditions under which the creation of wealth could be achieved most efficiently, and for this tendency towards totalitarianism to be resisted, then, it was necessary for 'The obstacles to the working of markets [...] to be ruthlessly removed'; 'The short-term pain in terms of unemployment, bankruptcies, and living standards' would be worth enduring to 'establish capitalism on a firm footing' (ibid.: 46). A central feature of Hayek's neoliberalism, therefore, is the need to create and re-create 'the widest possible conditions for markets to flourish, which means removing as many restrictions on competition as possible' (Gamble 2001: 131).

Hayek's justification for the removal of restrictions on competition is not limited to his observations about the links between planning and totalitarianism, but also extends to his concern for freedom. Hayek (2001 [1945]: 33) asks: 'Who can seriously doubt that the power which a millionaire, who may be an employer, has over me is very much less than that which the smallest bureaucrat possesses who wields the coercive power of the state and on whose discretion it depends how I am allowed to live and work?'

In privileging the freedom of people, which he believed is necessarily suppressed by centralized planning, Hayek (ibid.: 33) derives the opinion that an unskilled labourer in England has greater freedom than employers in Germany or highly skilled workers in Russia (in the 1930s and 1940s) because 'he faces no absolute impediments' to changing employment, residence or leisure pursuits: 'There are no dangers to bodily security and freedom that confine him by brute force to the task and environment to which a superior has assigned him.' It is the maintenance of this freedom which is imperative for Hayek, and he argues that it had been 'forgotten that the system of private property is the most important guarantee of freedom' because it is by virtue of the system of private property 'that we as individuals can decide what to do with ourselves' (ibid.: 33).

This understanding of the basis of freedom not only has implications for the status of private property, but also for the role of the state. This is because the state must act to ensure that there is a free economy to prevent the kind of curtailment of individual freedoms that produce suboptimal outcomes and tend towards totalitarianism, but also to protect the system of private property that allows for that freedom to be exercised by individuals. From this, we can infer that there is no need for redistribution or state provision to address inequalities in incomes and wealth. Hayek is not concerned so much with the contributions that different classes of people make to the creation of wealth and the justice of the distribution that the politico-legal structure provides for, as he is with how markets can be made to work most effectively, because it is this which contributes to the creation of wealth. Guaranteeing freedom and private property are necessary and sufficient conditions for this purpose because relevant information to help people adjust their plans is transmitted most effectively through the market and because the basis of private property requires an institutionalized system of law and justice. For Hayek, this means the establishment of the Rule of Law, which gives all actors certainty about the conditions under which they may use their property, and allows them to plan their action under the state's protection from arbitrary interventions by other individuals or the government itself (ibid.: 49–51). In other words, Hayek believed that the state must be strong because the market's existence is dependent on the state's ability to create the conditions for it to function.

This discussion of Hayek has shown how he believed the best economic outcomes to be the product of the efficient use of knowledge transmitted through the price system in a competitive market, and how he believed that planning against competition rather than planning for competition (ibid.: 38) would tend towards totalitarian government, which all people of a good character would reject. Planning *for* competition, however, was seen as an intrinsic feature of the state's role. From here, it is possible to draw the conclusion that the state should offer nothing more than the fierce protection of private property and free markets. Given that Hayek believed planning cannot take place without tending towards totalitarianism, the fact that the market distributes resources in a way that means those who are less deserving may receive greater rewards than those who are more deserving is a secondary point. As Gamble (1996b: 47) notes: 'Hayek is not shocked by this. He argues that it cannot be otherwise.'

However, as was the case with Adam Smith's work, it is important not to overstate the case, and there is a second kind of security that Hayek believed is compatible with the necessary freedom that the economy requires to produce market equilibrium. Hayek (2001 [1945]: 58) refers to this as 'the certainty of a given minimum of sustenance for all'. He argued that there could be no reason why 'in a society which has reached the general level of wealth ours has [that this] kind of security should not be guaranteed to all [...] that is: some minimum of food, shelter and clothing, sufficient to preserve health' (ibid.: 59). Here, then, we can see Hayek arguing for a state that acts as a minimal social safety net as well as a guarantor of the conditions which allow the market to reach equilibrium: namely, the removal of barriers to the operation of the free market, and the rigorous protection of private property. As Gamble (1996a: 51) noted: 'Hayek wished to restrict the role of government to a minimum. However, to the dismay of many libertarians he identified numerous areas where it was legitimate for government to have a role [...] the real issue is where the line should be drawn, not whether a line should be drawn at all.'

The Hayekian state that is 'charged with responsibilities in education, health, and many other fields, as well as ensuring a minimum standard of income' (ibid.: 51), therefore raises some interesting questions in the context of Hayek's concern not for the justice of the social relations that produce wealth in capitalism as such, but for the way in which those social relations can be made to operate most efficiently.

Hayek's principal concern was about how markets could be made to work most effectively – to reach equilibrium – since this is how wealth is created and expanded most effectively. He thought that competition and the price system were the most efficient ways of filtering relevant knowledge, and that planning against competition rather than planning for competition would inevitably lead to totalitarianism. In stark contrast to Keynes, then, Hayek's understanding of capitalism suggests that the role of the state should be limited to the protection of private property and people's fundamental freedoms, and while he acknowledged that this would create inequality, he did not believe that capitalism could be made to operate in any other way.

Conclusion

This chapter has outlined four ways in which it is possible to understand capitalism. In Smith, we see the possibility for optimum outcomes stemming from the exchange of equivalents between equals, while in Marx we see the exploitation of one group of people by another. For Keynes, suboptimal outcomes can be addressed through state action, whereas for Hayek they can be resolved only by the market. The differing implications for the institutional arrangements governing society that stem from these theories are stark. Smith imagined a state that needs to create conditions for the free exchange of goods; Marx, a state that subordinates the interests of workers to capitalists; for Keynes, the state should intervene to offset the problems of depression, while Hayek believed that such intervention was the reason that markets did not operate to their full potential, and that the state should simply plan for competition. These different approaches to understanding wealth in capitalism therefore demonstrate clearly how our perceptions of how the economy operates can play a key role in informing how we believe that it should be organized and governed. In turn, these ideas contribute to the way in which we, as individuals in society, decide to contribute to making, remaking or resisting capitalism.

2 | CAPITALISM AND ITS CRISES

Introduction

The previous chapter outlined four differing ways in which capitalism has been understood in a theoretical sense, focusing on the work of Smith, Marx, Keynes and Hayek. The central argument of the chapter was that the way in which we understand the process of accumulating wealth has fundamental significance for how we judge the merits of the capitalist form of social and economic organization. This chapter assesses the varying understandings of capitalist social relations discussed in Chapter 1 in relation to their ability to account for crises in capitalism, and begins with a historical examination of three specific crises of capitalism: the interwar collapse and the Great Depression; the collapse of the Bretton Woods system and the 1970s stagflation; and the sub-prime mortgage crisis of the late 2000s.

The chapter shows how the relationship between the state and the economy during the interwar collapse, the collapse of Bretton Woods and the sub-prime crisis broadly reflected the views of the relationship between state and market envisaged by Smith, Keynes and Hayek respectively. However, it will show how the 'laissez-faire', 'Keynesian' and 'neoliberal' state forms were unable to insulate the international economy from crisis, with profound social consequences. On this basis, the chapter argues that capitalism displays an *inherent tendency towards crises*. The final section of the chapter is dedicated to explaining the social basis of this inherent tendency towards crisis, which, it suggests, lies in capital's contradictory relationship with labour. If different ways of attempting to manage capitalism, which broadly reflected the understandings of capitalism put forward by Smith, Keynes and Hayek, have shown themselves to be inadequate, the theoretical proposition that capitalism itself is inherently crisis-prone gathers empirical weight. As such, the chapter argues that there is a powerful rationale for an alternative to capitalism that emerges from an understanding of capitalism as an inherently crisis-prone form of social organization.

The interwar collapse and the Great Depression

The late nineteenth and early twentieth centuries were the halcyon days of laissez-faire liberalism, and can be characterized in terms of the generalized belief (among advanced economies) in free trade, and the notion that the role of the state should be limited to the creation of conditions for the benefits of free trade to be realized. Broadly reflecting the ideas of Adam Smith, it was thought that if this could be achieved, there would be gains to be made by everybody. However, ultimately the period displayed contradictions in its overarching framework in the form of the Gold Standard, the consequences of which were amplified by the trauma of the Wall Street Crash.

Laissez-faire in general, and free trade in particular, was facilitated by a number of factors, including British naval superiority, which was able to provide security for the transit of goods between differing territories. However, the most significant overarching characteristic of the laissez-faire period was the exchange rate regime – known as the Gold Standard – that served to significantly reduce the transaction costs associated with international trade. In particular, it was able to remove the need to transport bulky precious metals to finance international transactions by instilling trust in national currencies through its establishment of an agreed, stable relationship between national currencies and gold. The Gold Standard therefore represented a set of agreed rules that related each national currency to an internationally accepted monetary standard, and provided public and private institutions with the confidence to engage in international trade. In a reflection of the liberal belief that all countries would benefit from free trade, the maintenance of the institutions that facilitated it was afforded the highest priority by policy-makers.

The Gold Standard had two key operational features. First, each national currency had a fixed value in terms of gold, and national central banks would guarantee to convert their currency into gold at that rate. This meant that people could trade with confidence that the currencies they were using reflected a commonly accepted standard of value, and that a country could not increase the supply of its currency without undermining its gold reserves and hence its ability to engage in future trade. Secondly, currencies were able to change in value in relation to one another. This allowed prices to reflect changes in the supply and demand of goods and services that were traded, but only within certain limits, because national central banks were constrained in how far they could let their currency fall in value in relation to other currencies by their commitment to exchange currency for gold at the fixed rate. As such, the Gold Standard was seen to represent a system that could provide countries with the confidence to trade with one another, and which could automatically serve to keep the balance of international trade in equilibrium.

The theoretical operation of the system can be illustrated with a brief example of a two-currency economy. At the beginning of the trading relationship, the value of each currency is fixed in terms of gold but variable in terms of the other. For example, 1 ounce of gold is equal to £1 and US$1, and £1 is equal to US$1. However, when there is a change in the trading relationship stemming from a change in British demand for goods from the United States, exchange rates must shift. This is because in order to buy the newly popular goods, it is necessary for British people to buy the requisite foreign currency – in this case US dollars – and Americans need an incentive to sell them. This allows them to demand a higher price for dollars. In the new scenario, 1 ounce of gold is still equal to £1 and US$1; however, it costs £1.50 to buy US$1. If an individual were to exchange US$10 (which is worth 10 ounces of gold) for £15, they could use this £15 to buy 15 ounces of gold, transport this back to the United States, and exchange this for US$15. They would therefore make a profit of US$5, minus the costs of transporting the gold from Britain to the United States. As gold leaves the reserves of Britain, the central bank must respond if the credibility of the fixed rate is not to be undermined. As such, it must reduce the money supply by removing currency from circulation or raising interest rates to limit new borrowing, which reduces demand for imported goods. The lower demand for US$ then means that the rate of exchange between sterling and the US dollar returns to £1 equal to US$1 (the example is summarized from O'Brien and Williams 2010: Box 4.1, pp. 98–9; for other discussions, see also Lairson and Skidmore 2003: 53; Baylis et al. 2011: 453; Kettell 2004: 33–5).

The Gold Standard is therefore significant because its successful operation was dependent on the ability of individual states to impose deflation on their domestic economies when the terms of trade shifted against them, which Britain felt independently of any moment of acute economic crisis in the 1920s. As Steven Kettell (2004: 34) noted, Britain had adopted the Gold Standard in 1821 and most of the world subscribed to it by the 1880s. At this time, £1 could buy 113 grains of fine gold, which was equivalent to US$4.86, 'establishing a parity between the two currencies of £1=$4.86 or $1=£0.205'. However, the system was suspended during and immediately after the First World War as Britain sought to ensure it could finance its military expenditure and post-war reconstruction by using credit monies to purchase essential goods and services overseas. This meant that at the end of the war, the ratio of pounds in circulation to gold had vastly increased; if the Gold Standard had been in operation and everyone tried to convert their pounds to gold at the same time at the fixed rate (as guaranteed by the Gold Standard), Britain would not be able to meet its obligations. If Britain was to return to the Gold Standard and avoid a catastrophic gold drain that would prevent it from trading, it would need to reduce the supply of money in circulation in order to be able to meet its Gold Standard commitments. This would have significant knock-on effects in terms of unemployment until the economy had returned to competitiveness at the prevailing exchange rates, and Britain began to experience inflows of gold that allowed it to once again expand the money supply.

Not only had the ratio of pounds to gold become unbalanced during the suspension of the Gold Standard, but British industries had become increasingly uncompetitive because they had neglected to renew shop-floor skills, and capital investment abroad had outstripped domestic investment threefold in the period 1870–1913 (Dintenfass 1992: 41). Following the First World War, Britain found that markets it had neglected during the war had turned to the United States and Japan to meet demand for goods and services (Eichengreen 1996: 69). Britain had also accumulated some £6 billion of debt plus additional interest charges during the war, and the domestic political situation meant that this amount could not be financed through taxation or current savings (Tomlinson 1990: 50–1). It seemed clear that any attempt to restore the Gold Standard in its pre-war form would fail because of Britain's changed circumstances in relation to its competitors in the global economy. However, in 1925 Britain nonetheless decided to return to the Gold Standard at the pre-war rate of £1 = US$4.86, which meant its industries were not competitive internationally, and without an improvement in British competitiveness, a contraction in Britain's money supply or an expansion in the supply of money in countries accumulating gold, Britain's gold reserves would be depleted.

In the pre-war period, when Britain had been at the centre of the international monetary system, the Bank of England had managed the Gold Standard to prevent 'sustained inflows and sustained outflows of gold' (Bernanke and James 1991: 38). In other words, it responded to changes in the terms of trade by contracting and expanding the money supply as and when circumstances required. This meant that when changes in the terms of trade occurred, adjustment could occur without any nation having to suffer from prolonged periods of deflation. In the interwar period, however, Britain was no longer at the centre of the international monetary system, and the United States and France 'had central banks with little or no incentive to avoid accumulation of gold' (ibid.: 38). This meant that the deflationary bias of the Gold Standard became more prolonged and exacting on any state that suffered adversely, as Britain had, from a shift in the terms of trade.

The Gold Standard therefore had an inbuilt deflationary bias that needed careful management if it was to operate as it was intended, and as it had in the pre-war period. However, the changed circumstances of the interwar period, in which countries had returned to the Gold Standard at pre-war parities despite fundamental changes in their competitive positions and where there was an absence of monetary leadership that could serve to offset the deflationary bias of the Gold Standard system, meant that countries could find themselves exposed to prolonged periods of deflation if they were to avoid a gold drain that would undermine their ability to trade. In turn, this would have important social implications in the form of unemployment, as the reduced supply of money translated itself into lower demand for goods and services, and therefore the people that provided them.

Despite the deflationary bias of the interwar Gold Standard, the 1920s had nonetheless been a decade of prosperity, founded on the dual bases of property speculation and stock market speculation, which reflected people's desire to accumulate wealth. As John Kenneth Galbraith (2009 [1955]: 32) noted, 1920s America saw people 'displaying an inordinate desire to get rich quickly with a minimum of physical effort'. If these foundations were shaken, the consequences of the deflationary bias in the Gold Standard framework would be amplified as upward pressure on unemployment increased, and this is precisely what occurred. This proved problematic because of the precariousness of speculation. For instance, throughout the 1920s, land in areas like Florida 'was gaining in value by the day and could be sold at a handsome profit in a fortnight' (ibid.: 33), even though the intrinsic value of the property traded became increasingly dubious for reasons ranging from the quality of the land to outright fraud. This was increasingly realized by investors who found themselves in possession of worthless land, and demand began to taper off, so that by 'the spring of 1926, the supply of new buyers, so essential to the reality of increasing house prices, began to fall' (ibid.: 34).

A similar picture was repeated in the stock market, as strong business performances in the early 1920s had resulted in increasing share prices, with the New York Times share index more than doubling between 1924 and 1927 (ibid.: 36). The market activity was exacerbated by the widespread use of margin trading – whereby share purchases are financed through borrowing so the buyer can benefit from the increase in value of stock without making the sacrifices of an initial outlay. Investment banks and their subsidiaries also contributed to inflating stock prices by investing in their own shares. In one such instance, Galbraith (ibid.: 86) notes how the Goldman Sachs Trading Corporation, a subsidiary of Goldman Sachs, purchased over half a million shares in its own stock for some US$57 million, which had 'boomed their value'. This subsidiary then launched its own investment trust with no physical assets other than the capital invested in it by stockholders, buoyed by the faith in the rising stock price of the parent firm. With no discernible assets, the vast riches being acquired amounted to little more than a house of cards, which collapsed in spectacular fashion in October 1929. Stocks in the Goldman Sachs Trading Corporation that had been trading at US$1.04 in 1928 were valued at US$0.0125 at the time of Senate hearings on the Wall Street Crash held in 1932 (ibid.: 90).

While this speculation had been occurring, the deflationary bias of the Gold Standard that existed because of the lack of monetary leadership began to assert itself more readily as the United States introduced deflationary policies in 1928 to try to curb stock market speculation, despite the fact that it was experiencing gold inflows and would have been expected to inflate its economy to avoid imposing a deflationary burden on other countries (Bernanke and James 1991: 39–40). France, the other major country experiencing inflows of gold, similarly failed to inflate its economy, and partly because of 'restrictions on open market operations' and partly 'because of deliberate policy choices [...] the country actually experienced a wholesale price *deflation* of 11% between January 1929 and January 1930' (ibid.: 40, emphasis in original).

As the precariousness of the two pillars of interwar economic prosperity was exposed, and in the absence of clear economic leadership, the deflationary bias of the Gold Standard system began to assert itself in a scramble for gold that was characterized by self-reinforcing competitive deflations (ibid.: 40). In the process, unemployment throughout the world increased and there were increasing calls for protection for workers from the state. One of the forms that this took in the United States was the introduction of the Smoot-Hawley Tariff Act, which introduced tariffs on over twenty thousand imported goods, and which reduced American imports by up to one third. As decline for goods and services from overseas was felt, unemployment elsewhere increased and governments responded competitively in order to try to offset the social consequences of the deflationary spiral that had been set in motion. Ultimately, this deflationary bias, the speculative nature of interwar economic prosperity in the United States, the absence of leadership in the international monetary system, and the competition between states that it provoked saw the world economy enter the Great Depression.

In light of the fact that the restoration of the laissez-faire liberal state form in the interwar period had proved unable to create conditions that allowed everybody to benefit from free trade facilitated by the Gold Standard, Karl Polanyi (2001 [1944]) argued that it was necessary to consider the foundations of laissez-faire liberalism more closely. He noted, in particular, how the operation of the system was not simply dependent on states creating conditions for free trade through their maintenance of the Gold Standard. Rather, the system was also dependent on the commodification of labour, land and money, which are fundamental to the production, distribution and exchange of goods.

Polanyi (ibid.: 76) described these commodities as fictitious commodities on the grounds that they are not created for sale, but are redescriptions of nature, people and means of payment. However, under capitalist production they are nonetheless treated as commodities to be used or discarded as circumstances require, and if they are treated as such, there will necessarily be undesirable consequences. As Polanyi phrased it, labour 'cannot be shoved about, used indiscriminately, or even left unused, without affecting also the human individual who happens to be the bearer of that particular commodity' (ibid.: 76). Land likewise bears the consequences of use as its productivity (and therefore the ability to produce food) is affected by levels of grazing and fallow time (ibid.: 76). For money to function, people must be able to trust it as a store of value and means of payment: 'shortages and surfeits of money would prove as disastrous to business as floods and droughts in primitive societies' (ibid.: 76).

In order for the economy to operate harmoniously, therefore, Polanyi argued, economic relations had to be 'embedded' in their social and political contexts – that is to say, the way in which the economy operated had to appreciate the impact that it had on the natural elements on which it relied. However, the deflationary bias of the Gold Standard did not provide for this, and in the absence of decisive leadership in the monetary system, actually served to progressively undermine the sustainability of the fictitious commodities of labour, land and money. In the process, their status as fictitious commodities showed that they could not be subjected to management by the technicalities of the Gold Standard, and would require government intervention in order to prevent them from being destroyed. In other words, the laissez-faire period inevitably saw an 'extension of market organization in respect to genuine commodities' that 'was accompanied by its restriction in respect to fictitious ones' (ibid.: 76); as Andrew Gamble (2009: 52) has summarized, for Polanyi, 'setting economic activity free had led to huge inequalities and suffering in society, and in time had produced strong political reaction' to counter it.

The reason that this ultimately led to a serious crisis was the fact that the measures necessary to provide social protection in response to the impact of the market on labour, land and money were incompatible with the laissez-faire system of free trade. For Polanyi (2001 [1944]: 147), then, 'while laissez-faire economy was the product of deliberate State action, subsequent restrictions on laissez-faire started in a spontaneous way. Laissez-faire was planned; planning was not.' Polanyi (ibid.: 21) therefore conceived of the interwar collapse as a startling intellectual failure.

> To liberal economists the gold standard was a purely economic institution; they refused to even consider it as part of a social mechanism. Thus it happened that the democratic countries were the last to realize the true nature of the catastrophe and the slowest to counter its effects. Not even when the cataclysm was already upon them did their leaders see that behind the collapse of the international system there stood a long development within the most advanced countries that made that system anachronistic ...

This interpretation of the Gold Standard has become widely shared among economic historians and political economists, and this consensus has been aptly captured by John Gerard Ruggie (1982: 387), who poignantly suggested that 'it was the singular tragedy of the interwar period [...] to have attempted to restore internationally, in the form of the gold-exchange standard in particular, that which no longer had a corresponding social base domestically'.

The laissez-faire liberal state form, from which the interwar collapse and the onset of the Great Depression emerged, can be clearly associated with the acceptance of the political economy of Adam

Smith. Just as Smith had argued that everybody could gain from the division of labour and free trade if the state created conditions to facilitate it, the laissez-faire era was predicated upon the belief that focusing all policy objectives on the maintenance of the system of free trade through the Gold Standard would provide for prosperity. However, the impact of the deflationary bias in the operation of the Gold Standard that asserted itself catastrophically following the Wall Street Crash, and in light of an absence of clear leadership in the international monetary system, suggests that the laissez-faire liberal state form cannot account for crisis in capitalism, and as such could not provide a basis for stability.

The break-up of Bretton Woods and the 1970s stagflation

In 1944, representatives of the allied powers met at Bretton Woods, New Hampshire, in order to discuss the reconstruction of the international monetary system after the Second World War. Conscious of the devastating effects of the deflationary bias of the Gold Standard in the absence of strong monetary leadership, the leading negotiators, Harry Dexter White of the United States, and John Maynard Keynes of Great Britain, sought a solution that could both provide a system of stable exchange rates that would ensure confidence to promote international trade, and give governments enough flexibility to pursue domestic objectives, including full employment (De Vries 1986: 11; Rogers 2012: 3; Ruggie 1982: 388). With such a solution, governments would be able to respond to domestic political pressures without simply offsetting the costs of economic adjustment to other nations in a way that had not been possible during the interwar years. In recognizing the importance of full employment, the system resonated with Keynes' conception of how capitalism operated.

The post-war period is often referred to as the era of 'embedded liberalism'. Through the institutionalization of economic relations established by the Bretton Woods system, its aim was to create a permissive environment that would legitimize the pursuit of full employment by states, by insulating them from the pressures of the financial markets. As Ruggie (1982: 393) has phrased it, the post-war order 'would be multilateral in character; unlike the liberalism of the gold standard and free trade, its multilateralism would be predicated on domestic interventionism'. While there may have been differences between the views of the Bretton Woods negotiators about the technical details of the proposals, Ruggie (ibid.: 393–4) argues that 'they shared a common purpose; intergovernmental collaboration to facilitate balance-of-payments equilibrium, in an international environment of multilateralism and a domestic context of full employment'.

Like the Gold Standard, the Bretton Woods agreement contained provisions for a fixed exchange rate regime to provide stability and confidence in international trade. However, unlike the Gold Standard, the new exchange rate regime would have provisions for adjustments in instances where economic imbalances were deemed to be so fundamental that they would not adjust naturally over time. These adjustments would be overseen and authorized by the International Monetary Fund, thereby preventing the pursuit of competitive beggar-thy-neighbour policies that had stemmed from the deflationary biases of the Gold Standard and contributed to the onset of the Great Depression (see, *inter alia*, Bergsten 2005: 376; Krueger 1998: 1984–5; Rogers 2012: 4). The keystone of the system would be convertibility of the US dollar into gold at a rate of $35 per ounce, as the United States found itself the world's leading creditor after the Second World War. All other currencies were to be fixed against the dollar at a given exchange rate, known as a par-value. In order to oversee and facilitate the operation of the system, the IMF would carry out routine surveillance operations in all of its member countries to assess the sustainability of the par-value, and if it thought that existing policies were not sustainable, the IMF could make recommendations to domestic policy-makers, who would be under no obligation to accept this advice. If a country's economic difficulties persisted, but it was felt that they were of a transitory nature, the IMF would lend resources to bridge the gap until an adjustment in domestic policy had brought the system back into balance. In a worst-case scenario, where the economy was deemed to be fundamentally out of balance, the IMF could authorize a change in the par-value of a currency.

In providing governments with room for manoeuvre to respond to demands for domestic full employment, the system hoped to avoid the consequences of the deflationary biases of the Gold Standard by re-establishing the compatibility of economic relations with their social and political contexts. The system formally came into existence in 1946, but was initially beset by problems, as the par-values set proved to be 'unsustainable throughout 1947 and 1948, and as a result had to be adjusted in a widespread devaluation' (Rogers 2012: 4). Shortly after this, in 1950, Canada abandoned its par-value, while France, Greece and Italy did not even set par-values until the late 1950s and early 1960s (De Vries 1986: 43–64; Rogers 2012: 4), and in the 1950s Britain considered abandoning its par-value in order to depreciate the pound and assist the competitiveness of British industry (Grant 2002: 23; Burnham 2003). However, despite these initial teething problems, the par-value system survived without the departure of any leading members until the early 1970s.

Throughout this period, however, the system began to show signs of stress, which stemmed from expansionary fiscal policy in the United States and evolutions in global finance. The first phase of this occurred throughout the 1950s as increasing amounts of American dollars were accumulated outside of the United States. A number of factors contributed to this. First, the demands of post-war reconstruction had meant many European economies found themselves short of the American dollars that they needed to pay for necessary goods and services. However, the United States had responded to this problem by embarking on a programme of lending to European economies in the form of the Marshall Plan, alongside continuing large-scale military expenditures. The result of these policy measures was a transition from a global dollar shortage to a global dollar glut. For as long as holdings of dollars overseas did not exceed the United States' gold reserves at a rate of US$35 per ounce, the system would be stable. However, as early as 1958 the United States' gold reserves had fallen below overseas dollar holdings, and it could no longer meet its guarantee to exchange dollars for gold at a rate of US$35 per ounce. This situation was known as the 'Triffin Dilemma', after the Belgian-American economist Robert Triffin, who first identified it. As Ruggie (1982: 407, fn 91) explains:

if the United States corrected its balance of payments deficit, the result would be world deflation because gold production at $35 an ounce could not adequately supply world monetary reserves. But if the United States continued running a deficit, the result would be the collapse of the monetary standard because U.S. foreign liabilities would far exceed its ability to convert dollars into gold on demand.

The anchor of the system had therefore been compromised by the massive expansion of world trade financed by American dollars.

The problem of the Triffin Dilemma was amplified by evolutions in global finance, and particularly the evolution of the Eurodollar markets, in which banks outside of the United States began lending in dollars, thus undermining the ability of the US Federal Reserve to control the supply of dollars to the world economy through its monetary policy. In turn, this further undermined the ability of the United States to meet its obligations to exchange dollars for gold at the agreed rate of US$35 per ounce (see ibid.: 407–8; Rogers 2012: 7–8). Despite ongoing discussions about ways in which the system might be reformed (see Triffin 1969), by 1971 American dollar liabilities so far exceeded the country's gold reserves at the fixed rate of US$35 per ounce that the American president, Richard Nixon, unilaterally decided to suspend the dollar's convertibility into gold.

The fact that the system's anchor had been undermined by as early as 1958 and had been removed by 1971 was not the only problem faced by the Bretton Woods system, because despite the incorporation of capital controls in the Bretton Woods framework to prevent speculative capital transactions, such transactions had begun to steadily increase throughout the 1950s (Cohen 1996: 268). In combination with the collapse of the par-value system and the shift to floating rates, this meant that governments were once again exposed to the pressure of financial markets, which appeared to make it impossible for them to maintain their monetary policy autonomy and currency stability in the context of convertibility (Andrews 1994; Cohen 1996, 1998). This became increasingly significant in the context of the widely shared belief that the pursuit of full employment was a legitimate aim of government policy.

In the United Kingdom, this acceptance had ushered in a period of apparent consensus between all of the major political parties on the desirability of using state expenditure to promote full employment and certain other social objectives, which has been described as the 'Keynesian Revolution' in economic policy (see Booth 1983), although others have questioned its existence (Matthews 1968; Tomlinson 1981, 1984). Along with historically high levels of investment (Matthews 1968), the system of 'embedded liberalism' had allowed governments to increase their expenditure to support aggregate demand without worrying about the response of financial markets and the consequences that this would have for the exchange rate and levels of foreign reserves. In the context of floating rates and increasing financial transactions, however, these concerns again became significant, especially as full employment had placed upward pressure on wages and attempts to curb union power had proved unsuccessful. The power of the union movement also resulted in pressure on the government to increase expenditure on other social objectives, which further contributed to inflationary pressures. In a context in which much of British industry remained uncompetitive because of the prevalence of collusive industrial behaviour that subdued competition and research and development (Broadberry and Crafts 2001: 99), these pressures saw Britain persistently in a state of deficit, faced with rising inflation.

This situation was also exacerbated by external events, and most notably increases in the cost of oil imposed by the Organization of the Petroleum Exporting Countries (OPEC). The abandonment of dollar convertibility and 'devaluations of the dollar in terms of gold in December 1971 and February 1973 [had] reduced the receipts of oil exporting countries [...] by as much as fifteen per cent' (De Vries 1985: 307), and gave an incentive to raise prices. Hostilities in the Middle East and oil embargoes on countries that showed strong, overt support for Israel (ibid.: 306) exacerbated supply problems, resulting in a fourfold increase in the cost of oil between the beginning of October 1973 and the beginning of January 1974 (ibid.: 308). As Ian Skeet (1988: 58) argued, there was no escaping the impact of the OPEC price increases. Not only did they mean that there would be massive payments imbalances as dollars flowed to oil-exporting countries that did not have the capacity to spend them on imported goods, they also meant that the very basis of the post-war economic boom – the 'availability of abundant cheap energy' (ibid.: 305) – had disappeared (on this point, see also Childs 1979: 237).

The advanced economies therefore found themselves faced with a number of issues; governments were confronted with price inflation that stemmed from the strength of the labour movement that had been facilitated by the generalized acceptance of full employment as a legitimate aim of government policy; price inflation was exacerbated by the increased cost of oil; the structural balance of payments deficits caused by oil price increases caused a global contraction of demand that increased unemployment, and in turn led to further calls for public expenditure to support jobs.

In the late 1950s, the prevailing paradigm of economic policy-making – Keynesianism – had adopted a belief (it was not a view held by Keynes himself) that there was a stable long-run trade-off between inflation and unemployment that meant lower unemployment could effectively be purchased with a slightly higher rate of inflation, which could in turn be limited by allowing unemployment to rise. However, as governments spent money to try to bring unemployment down, they found that not only did inflation continue to increase, but reductions in the level of unemployment proved to be only temporary. They were therefore faced simultaneously with rising levels of unemployment, rising levels of inflation, and rising levels of public debt. This was the previously unknown phenomenon of 'stagflation', which called into question the Keynesian intellectual foundations of post-war economic policy-making (see Hall 1993).

In response to these anomalies, monetarists like Milton Friedman (1976: 15) began to argue that there is 'no stable trade-off between inflation and unemployment; there is a natural rate of unemployment'. The implication of the argument was that a reduction in unemployment caused by an inflationary expansion in the supply of money will only last a short period of time before unemployment rises back to its natural level, while inflation remains at the higher rate. This is because people demand wages on the basis of the *real* wage rate (the wage rate relative to prices), which also determines the demand for labour (Friedman 1975: 15). In other words, because levels of wages and employment are functions of the *real* value of wages, increases in their *nominal* value will produce only short-lived gains while the market adjusts to the new *real* wage rate.

In empirical terms, David Laidler (1976: 488) attributed the apparent success of Keynesian demand management to the fixed-rate system. He argued that because exchange rates were fixed, inflation was reflected in periodic balance of payments crises (where industries were uncompetitive at prevailing world prices) rather than a fall in the exchange rate. As he phrased it, the world economy took the strain because 'domestic inflation cannot forever deviate from that ruling in the world economy' (ibid.: 488; Laidler 1975). Devaluations under the fixed-rate regime were therefore now interpreted as a product of inflationary monetary expansion designed to reduce the rate of unemployment. As Ball and Burns (1976: 476) noted: 'Sterling was devalued in November [1967] in the mistaken belief that the inability to combine the target unemployment rate with an adequate current account performance was due entirely to an incorrect exchange rate rather than a mistaken unemployment rate.'

In other words, the permissive environment created by the Bretton Woods system allowed countries to pursue expansionary fiscal policy, but only at the cost of inflation, which both undermined the foundations of the Bretton Woods exchange rate regime and had no discernible lasting impact on unemployment.

The phenomenon of stagflation therefore resulted in the emergence of a new intellectual paradigm of economic policy-making that suggested it was not possible for governments to intervene in the economy with fiscal policy in order to promote full employment. Furthermore, in the context of increasing international capital transactions, the markets were once again able to assert discipline on governments suffering from high public expenditure, high inflation and stagnant growth through currency speculation. This was felt most severely in the developed nations by Italy and the United Kingdom during the 1970s, when market reaction to levels of public expenditure deemed to be excessive led to persistent downward pressure on the lira and the pound respectively. Ultimately, both nations required financial support from the International Monetary Fund, and while measures were already being taken to limit the rate of growth of public expenditure and curtail the money supply, austerity and monetary discipline were entrenched in government policy through formal conditionality attached to the loans (see Burk and Cairncross 1992; Ludlam 1992; Rogers 2012). With the stagflation, and the shift in thinking about the state's role in facilitating full employment, the era of 'embedded liberalism' and the Keynesian mode of macroeconomic management that it had justified came to an end.

The period of embedded liberalism from which the 1970s stagflation emerged can clearly be associated with the principles of Keynesian political economy. Just as Keynes had argued that governments should intervene in the economy in times of uncertainty in order to bolster levels of employment and boost aggregate demand, embedded liberalism provided for interventionist state policy. However, throughout the period fiscal expansion and financial innovation served to undermine the basis of the par-value system and only temporarily alleviate unemployment at the cost of a permanently higher rate of inflation (which was exacerbated by the OPEC price increases). As governments in the Keynesian period of embedded liberalism were faced with rising unemployment, rising inflation, stagnant growth and rising public debt, it appears that Keynesian political economy cannot fully account for crises in capitalism, and as such could not provide a basis for stability.

The sub-prime crisis and the Great Recession

The austerity that began following the inability of Keynesian demand management to prevent crisis marked the beginning of the neoliberal era, which was consolidated with the election of Ronald Reagan as president of the United States and Margaret Thatcher's Conservative government in the United Kingdom. The intellectual landscape had already changed to favour minimal state intervention in the economy, and in the context of floating exchange rates and vastly increasing flows of speculative capital throughout the world economy, the room for manoeuvre for individual states to pursue policy autonomously came to appear increasingly limited as they were subjected to the discipline of international financial market confidence and the need to remain competitive.

As noted above, the increase in the scale of international financial transactions had begun in the Bretton Woods era with the growth of the Eurodollar markets; however, this process continued to a point where daily capital transactions represented 'five times the entire stock of money in the USA' by 1984 (Bienefeld 1992: 46). According to estimates by Richard Deeg and Mary A. O'Sullivan (2009: 731), by 2005 gross international capital flows had reached 16 per cent of GDP. Because the buying and selling of foreign currencies affects the exchange rates between currencies, and because the exchange rate between currencies affects individual nations' abilities to sell the goods and services they produce and buy the goods and services they need, this has important implications for governments.

Before the 1980s, exchange rates changed principally as a reflection of underlying trade balances – that is to say, exchange rates changed to reflect the relative value of goods and services produced in different countries. This meant that a fall in a country's exchange rate was an expression of a lack of competitiveness of its industries that could be addressed by restructuring, research and investment in new products, and so on. However, by the middle of the 1980s, this was no longer the case (Plender 1986: 40) because financial trades were increasingly made for the purposes of making profits from borrowing and lending in different currencies with different rates of interest (known as carry-trading) or from betting on whether the value of a currency would go up or down. If governments introduced policies that financial markets did not view favourably, they would face the prospect of speculation against their currencies, as Britain and Italy had in the 1970s.

As Peter Evans (1997: 63) noted, some scholars argued as a result of these developments that national states were undermined in favour of financial capital. However, it is far more common for emphasis to be placed on the way in which these developments changed the character of the relationship between states and markets. In the case of Canada, Manfred Bienefeld (1992: 31) argued that deregulation was part of the state's strategy to expose the domestic economy to competition to maximize efficiency and ensure the welfare of its citizens. More generally, it has been argued that the reforms to financial services represented a transformation of national states into 'competition states' in which governments aimed to secure their position in an international price hierarchy through exposure to competition. The '*sine qua non*' of the competition state, according to Phillip Cerny (1991: 74), 'is rapid adjustment to shifts in competitive advantage in the global marketplace'.

Financial globalization therefore made it appear that states were extremely limited in their room for manoeuvre, because if they engaged in expenditure that financial markets deemed to be imprudent, financial markets could discipline them. This meant that rather than providing for the needs of people by actively investing in jobs and welfare services, governments' roles were limited to creating conditions in which people could acquire the skills that they needed in order to find work and achieve prosperity in the global marketplace. In the language of Cerny (1997: 266), this represented 'competition states' giving up the 'decommodifying role' that they had played during the embedded liberal era under Bretton Woods, and taking on a 'marketizing role' that was more appropriate to the circumstances of globalization.

One of the consequences of this shift was the fact that government expenditure appeared to be legitimate only where it made a direct contribution to competitiveness. As such, this appeared to rule out extensive expenditure on social objectives like unemployment and housing benefits. In the United Kingdom, benefits of this kind were retained but made conditional on recipients showing their willingness to participate in the marketplace by actively seeking work. If people were unable to find work, they would be encouraged to participate in education and training in order to make them more competitive in the labour market, and therefore more able to contribute to national competitiveness at a point in the future. Reflecting the apparent constraints of financial globalization, after 1997 fiscal policy in the United Kingdom was therefore guided by two rules on expenditure: the first was that the government would spend only for the purposes of investment, and the second was that levels of expenditure would be prudent over the course of the economic cycle (see Balls 1998).

Governments therefore believed that financial globalization had clear implications for fiscal policy in general, and the extent to which they could spend on social policy in particular. However, it also had important implications for monetary policy, because financial markets were also concerned with the extent to which inflation could erode the value of their investments. This encouraged governments to take a tough anti-inflationary stance, and because it has been argued that politicians have a tendency to display 'time-inconsistent inflationary preferences' – that is to say that they are happy to see some inflation in the run-up to elections when it can boost electoral support – it became widely accepted that central bank independence was the most appropriate way for governments to keep inflation down (ibid.). However, this system reintroduced a deflationary bias to the economy as inflation was prioritized over all other economic objectives, and left governments with few policy tools with which to direct investment to areas that suffered from high unemployment (Hay 2001, 2004). From the point of view of governments, however, the situation was manageable politically because the consequences of attempts to achieve low inflation could be associated with the policy of the central bank responsible for setting interest rates, rather than the government itself (see Burnham 2001).

Under conditions where governments argued that they had no alternative but to reduce expenditure commitments and to prioritize the achievement of a low and stable rate of inflation to maintain market confidence, the question of how people could be provided with financial security in the absence of a state-funded social safety net became very important. However, the answer to this lay in encouraging individuals to invest in assets that would increase in value over time, and by increasing access to credit for the purposes of financing consumption. The former typically involved investment in equities and other financial assets through pension funds, and homeownership. The latter involved the use of short-term debt and especially credit card debt in order to allow people to maintain and increase their levels of consumption. Even in the context in which the developed nations were increasingly losing their competitive advantage to the newly industrializing countries, it was argued that it would be possible for people to maintain their levels of consumption during the completion of their transition towards high-skilled knowledge economies on the basis of the gains they made through their investments in property and other financial assets.

Colin Crouch (2009: 382) described the financialization of individuals as a system of 'Privatised Keynesianism', which was composed of 'a system of markets alongside extensive housing and other debt among low- and medium-income people linked to unregulated derivatives markets'. In other words, the social safety nets that had been provided by the state in the era of embedded liberalism would be replaced by the extension of credit, and could be sustained through financial innovation. Alan Finlayson (2009: 401) described this development as a transition towards a system of asset-based welfare that was reliant on the financialization of individuals and was 'intimately related to the reconfiguration of welfare states'. In other words, it was believed that although governments found themselves constrained in their ability to provide welfare services through their own expenditure by financial markets, if people were willing to take responsibility for their own well-being by engaging in education, training and employment, and investing in property and other financial assets, then the financial markets themselves would be able to provide security for people.

This system manifested itself in particular in the United States, where, Herman Schwartz (2008: 263) noted, 'cheap mortgages are financing the trenches defending against new demands for protection in the US and some other countries'. In other words, the housing market, and specifically the availability of cheap credit, was able to insulate the government from demands to provide the kinds of social expenditure that had been stripped back throughout the neoliberal period. The availability of such cheap credit in the United States was made possible in spite of the fact that the United States was the world's largest debtor nation, because the centrality of the dollar to the international monetary system meant that it nonetheless continued to attract large-scale inward investment. In 2005, Schwartz (ibid.: 264) noted, 'the US was like a private investor with debts totalling [$136 billion] and investments worth only [$111 billion], who somehow managed to pay out only [$45.41 billion] on those debts while receiving [$47.46 billion] on her own investments'. Because the demand for investment in the United States was so strong, the rate of interest that served as the basis on which mortgage rates were calculated remained low (ibid.: 246), and therefore created vast opportunities for American people to buy property. In the process, it also saw demand for property progressively inflate house prices, which allowed homeowners to borrow against the equity in their homes in order to further finance the purchase of consumer goods.

This situation would be sustainable as long as interest rates stayed low and house prices kept rising. However, in 2006 house prices in the United States reached their peak and began to decline in the face of 'significant excess supply of family houses. Inventories of vacant homes for sale, both new and existing, were rising. The number of buyers willing to bet on continued house price increases proved insufficient to absorb the inventories' (Jarsulic 2010: 33). This problem was particularly acute because throughout the housing boom there had been a significant extension of mortgage finance to 'subprime' borrowers, who 'are perceived to pose a higher than normal risk of default' because they have poor credit histories or have a high ratio of debt to income (ibid.: 3). When house prices had been rising, these borrowers were able to avoid default because they were able to use the increased equity in their homes resulting from rising house prices to either pay off their loans or refinance.

However, in the face of declining house prices, owner-occupiers were no longer able to rely on increasing equity in their homes to pay off mortgages or to refinance them, and as such the rate of defaults and foreclosures on properties began to increase, and in the process created 'a self-reinforcing cycle' as 'Foreclosures increased the stock of existing homes that are vacant and for sale' (ibid.: 33). By 2006, financial institutions had issued US$600 billion of sub-prime mortgages to borrowers deemed to have a high risk of default, and a further US$400 billion to borrowers who had self-certified their income because they were self-employed (ibid.: 23–5).

The system had been facilitated by the repeal of the Glass-Steagall Act. The Act, introduced in 1933, had forced financial institutions 'to decide whether they wanted to be in the securities business or the banking business' (Subramaniam 2011: 345), but on its repeal created new opportunities for firms to make money from sub-prime lending. One of the principal ways in which this occurred was through securitization, as firms engaged in investment banking repackaged sub-prime mortgages into Collateralized Debt Obligations (CDOs). These CDOs were comprised of many residential mortgages and divided into different tranches of risk, and were underwritten by the income streams of the underlying mortgages. That is to say, holders of CDOs received income from the repayment of the mortgages that they were constituted of, with the different tranches of the CDO receiving income according to their risk profile. As such, the upper tranches were the first to receive income, followed by the middle 'mezzanine' tranches, and lastly the 'equity' tranches. This structure allowed for the highest tranches of CDOs to be rated as AAA, the 'mezzanine' tranches to be rated as BBB, and 'equity' tranches to be unrated, providing markets for various investors with different appetites for risk. This made CDOs very attractive instruments for investors and in itself generated demand for further sub-prime lending so that the mortgages could be used to back new CDOs. According to Moody's Ratings, nearly 50 per cent of the securities that it rated during 2005 were made up of sub-prime mortgages (see Jarsulic 2010: 24–9).

The logic behind securitization was that bundling mortgages together would reduce the statistical probability of default because the income streams of CDOs were dependent on the repayment of many mortgages rather than just one, and the probability that all mortgages would default simultaneously was low. The belief that it is possible to use statistics to hedge risk – what Marieke de Goede (2004) has described as the depoliticization of financial risk – was magnified by the creation of Credit Default Swaps (CDSs), which were insurance contracts against default on CDOs. This provided holders of CDOs with security against default, and meant that the system appeared to be able to balance the risks involved in securitization and make the probability of widespread losses minimal.

However, as house prices stopped rising and foreclosures on sub-prime mortgages increased, the income streams of CDOs began to fall and they were downgraded by the major ratings agencies. As the value of the assets investment banks held was called into question, it became increasingly difficult for them to access short-term funding to finance their day-to-day operations, which ultimately resulted in the bankruptcy of Bear Stearns and Lehman Brothers. This had knock-on consequences throughout the financial system as the exposure of other banking institutions to toxic assets was called into question, and resulted in the British government's rescue of the Royal Bank of

Scotland and Lloyds TSB, as well as widespread intervention in the United States by the Federal Reserve, the Federal Deposit Insurance Corporation and the US Treasury. According to one study, the size of the United States government's lending and investment in order to save the financial system amounted to US$29 trillion (Felkerson 2011). The foundations of the financial collapse of 2007 can be seen in the foundations of neoliberalism itself, because the belief that financial markets were efficient created the legal framework in which financialization and securitization could occur. However, the accepted belief that financial market activity placed binding constraints on governments' ability to pursue public expenditure or direct investment through its use of monetary policy, which was ceded to central banks, also demanded it. This is because the social safety nets that had previously been provided by the state needed to be replaced so that people would be able to continue to provide for themselves in their old age, and so levels of consumption could be maintained as the developed nations made the transition to high-wage, high-skill economies in the face of competition in manufacturing from the newly industrializing nations. Following the collapse of this system, the people who were most likely to be reliant on the welfare services that states had cut in the 1980s in response to the logic of neoliberalism have not been able to realize the benefits of financialization that they were promised as it is this same group of people who were most likely to be in low-income groups and suffer from foreclosure and negative equity. To add insult to this injury, in the name of crisis resolution, governments across Europe have introduced further austerity measures on the grounds of market confidence, which have consolidated the kind of contradictions within neoliberalism that played a significant role in creating the crisis.

The period since the 1980s saw a widespread belief that markets could operate efficiently if states created the conditions for them to do so, reflecting the traditions of Hayek's neoliberalism. This resulted in the liberalization of finance, which led states to introduce welfare retrenchment in order to sustain financial market confidence, and in turn necessitated financialization, which could be justified on the grounds that markets will operate efficiently if they are not subjected to the interference of states. However, the extension of securitization that led to the crisis after the collapse of the housing market clearly calls into question the ability of this framework to account for crisis. Just as was the case with the laissez-faire liberal and Keynesian state forms, then, social and economic organization based in the ideas of neoliberal political economy does not appear to be able to provide a framework for stability.

Crisis tendencies in capitalism

The previous three sections have offered a narrative of historical crises in capitalism, and suggested that these crises emerged out of the laissez-faire liberal, Keynesian and neoliberal state forms, which reflected the views about the creation of wealth in the economy developed by Adam Smith, John Maynard Keynes and Friedrich Hayek, which were discussed in Chapter 1. On the grounds that the forms of state that were suggested by these understandings of capitalist wealth creation were not able to produce stability, the chapter has argued that none is able to account for crisis in capitalism, and that none can provide for stability. This section argues that there is an *inherent tendency towards crisis* in capitalism, which stems from capital's simultaneous dependence on the reproduction and the destruction of living labour.

While liberal and neoliberal political economy both suggest that markets will reach equilibrium if states allow for them to operate efficiently, Keynesian political economy does allude to the fact that there is an inherent tendency towards crisis in capitalism. This stemmed from Keynes' observation that people and firms tend to save money during times of uncertainty, that this behaviour becomes self-reinforcing and ultimately leads to ever more money being withdrawn from circulation, before resulting in a depression. The notion that uncertainty plays an important role in causing crises is one that has been developed more recently by constructivist scholars in political economy, who have suggested that crises occur when there is a widespread feeling that the tools and mechanisms that people have at their disposal to try to realize their goals are seen as insufficient. Colin Hay (2001: 203, emphasis in original) has phrased it like this: crises are moments of decisive intervention that stem from '*a perception of the need to make a decisive intervention*'. Similarly, Wesley

Widmaier et al. (2007: 748, emphasis in original) have argued that crises are *events which agents intersubjectively interpret as necessitating change*. In other words, crises occur when there is a broadly shared feeling that the status quo no longer provides conditions in which the objectives people wish to pursue can be realized. Both the Keynesian and constructivist interpretations of the origins of crises are appealing because of their intuitive basis. However, in the sense that they say very little about the reasons why this kind of uncertainty arises or is resolved, they are also unsatisfying in terms of their ability to help us understand *specifically* capitalist crises; in some respects, 'ideas' in this framework act as a kind of *deus ex machina* to account for both the causes of and resolutions to crises (Rogers 2013). In the political economy of Karl Marx, however, there is a clear conception of crisis that can be derived logically from the labour theory of value, and which can account for *specifically* capitalist crises, and reveals an *inherent tendency* towards crises in capitalist social relations.

It was established in Chapter 1 that Marx believed that labour alone creates value, and that capitalists realize their profits by extracting surplus value from labourers, which can be defined as the difference between the value that the labour-power that capitalists purchase can create in a day's work, and the cost of its daily subsistence (its value). In order for this to occur, labourers need to be free to sell their labour-power and free from the means of subsistence, so that there is a sufficient supply of labour-power for capitalists to exploit and so that they may realize surplus value. It is possible to see, then, how labour is dependent upon capital because it relies on capital for the wages it requires in order to purchase its means of subsistence. However, in order for capital to increase its value and therefore exist as capital defined as value in motion, it is also dependent upon labour, because without labour it is not possible for capitalists to create surplus value.

This codependence between capital and labour occurs within a particular ethos of production in capitalism. Whereas liberal political economists had believed that consumption was the sole purpose of production, Marxist analysis has suggested that this is 'transparently false and patently absurd, immediately contradicted by the very existence of capitalism', the purpose of which 'is not consumption, but the appropriation of profit and the accumulation of capital' (Clarke 2001: 95). As Marx (1990 [1867]: 742) himself phrased it, the logic of capitalism is the logic of accumulation, driven by the mantra 'Accumulate, accumulate! That is Moses and the prophets'. Capitalism, he argues, is defined by the tendency for capitalists to engage in 'Accumulation for accumulation's sake, production for production's sake'.

Under conditions of competition and in the context of the tendency to engage in accumulation for accumulation's sake, this codependence between capital and labour is contradictory. In part, this stems simply from the nature of labour's double freedom, in which 'the first aspect of their freedom permits them, and the second aspect forces them, to sell their labour-power in order to survive' (Holloway 1992: 153). The discipline of starvation that the nature of this double freedom implies shows the codependence between capital and labour to be antagonistic, a relation of struggle. However, this struggle becomes progressively antagonistic in the face of competition as capitalists seek to accumulate, because they, 'unlike the ruling class in any previous class society, are constantly driven through competition to increase exploitation, to increase the amount of unpaid surplus labour that is pumped out of the direct producers' (ibid.: 165). In order to do this, capitalists seek to lengthen the working day, but this encounters absolute limits determined by the physical ability of workers to work. As a result, capital seeks to increase the efficiency of labour by introducing technology into the production process, which means that there is 'a relative rise in that part of the capital invested in constant capital (machinery and raw materials) and a relative fall in variable capital (the part of the capital invested in the purchase of labour-power)' (ibid.: 166).

The competition between capitalists and the tendency to engage in accumulation for accumulation's sake therefore have the consequence of 'constantly expelling from the production process, in relative terms, the only source of its own existence, living labour' (ibid.: 166). As Werner Bonefeld (1992: 112) has phrased it, the logic of competition 'forces upon each individual capital the necessity of expelling living labour from the process of production'. Therefore, there appears to be a fundamental contradiction in the social relations of capitalism which stems from capital's dependence on the reproduction of labour-power and its tendency to undermine the basis of its existence in the quest to accumulate, and leads to progressively antagonistic relations between classes.

However, the exacerbation of class antagonism within capitalist social relations is not the only manifestation of inherent crisis tendencies in capitalism. This is because as living labour is expelled from the production process, not only is the relative value of commodities produced reduced because labour alone creates value, but demand for commodities is reduced. In other words, the tendency to expel living labour from production not only undermines the basis of capital's existence, it also leads to the production of commodities for which there is no demand, and which as a result cannot realize their value in exchange – the sole purpose of the capitalist production process. This situation can be described as a crisis of overproduction of commodities that people do not need or cannot afford, and which go unsold. The beginnings of crisis, stemming from the antagonistic nature of labour and capital's codependence, manifest themselves in the form of excess inventories, idle machinery, surplus money capital, unemployment and falling rates of return (Harvey 2006: 195).

The emergence of overproduction, however, does not immediately manifest itself in a moment of acute economic difficulty, because the banking and credit systems can serve to temporarily absorb the increasing antagonism that stems from the contradictory character of capitalist social relations. As firms find a falling demand for their products in the face of overproduction, they begin to withdraw money from circulation in order to act as a buffer that will help them weather periods of crisis, which means that credit is required in order to allow production and consumption to continue (Clarke 2011 [1988]: loc. 1922). By facilitating continued productive activity when confronted with inventories of commodities that cannot realize their value in exchange, credit 'appears to have the magical power of suspending altogether the barriers to the accumulation of capital, providing new finance for new ventures, and sustaining unprofitable capitalists and impoverished petty producers through periods of difficulty' (ibid.: loc. 2240).

Given the fact that credit allows both for the initial investment in the means of production, and its apparent ability to suspend barriers to accumulation, it appears to have the ability to 'straddle antagonisms to production and consumption, between production and realization, between present uses and future labour, between production and distribution' (Harvey 2006: 285–6).

However, this is little more than illusion. This is because, as Marx phrases it, just as 'money suspends the barriers of barter only by generalizing them [...] *credit* likewise suspends these barriers to the realization of capital only by raising them to their most general form' (Marx 1858). The speculative nature of the extension of credit can be revealed when we observe that debt is serviceable only 'on the expectation of some future extraction of surplus value' (Burnham 2011: 497). Rather than creating the conditions for the realization of surplus value that makes debt serviceable, however, credit serves to exacerbate the tendency towards crisis because for as long as it appears to overcome the contradictions in capitalist social relations, 'debts are regularly repaid, a mood of optimism prevails and credit becomes cheap and freely available'; therefore, it ultimately 'gives free reign to the tendency to the overaccumulation of capital' (Clarke, 2011 [1988]: loc. 2244).

David Harvey (2006: 301–5) has usefully illustrated the role of credit in relation to the crisis tendencies of capitalist social relations by outlining an 'accumulation cycle', which begins with a period of stagnation. In this period, there is a low demand for credit because people are uncertain about the prospects for generating future revenues, resulting in an excess of loanable capital relative to the opportunities for its productive employment. This period is followed by recovery, when opportunities created by the period of stagnation present themselves. For instance, surviving capitalists can purchase the assets of firms that did not weather the period of stagnation cheaply, reducing outlays on the means of production for firms that have survived. Because there is an excess of loanable money capital, interest rates are driven down and high levels of unemployment suppress wages, providing conditions that are 'optimal for financing long-term fixed capital formation'. In this period, capitalists generally have strong liquidity positions, which means they can extend commercial credit to one another from their cash reserves. This period is then followed by credit-based expansion. Bottlenecks between differing sectors of the economy created by the uneven nature of expansion during the period of recovery begin to appear, making it necessary to fund new investments to resolve them. As a result, the ability of firms to extend commercial credit to one another comes under strain, and firms must use funds loaned to them by banks. Following credit-based expansion there is speculative fever:

> Credit-based expansion generates price rises if only because the total quantity of circulating medium now far outstrips the product of social labour. In addition, unemployment disappears and wage rates begin to soar – the condition of labour, Marx observes, is always at its best on the eve of a crisis.

However, rising wages and rising interest rates that stem from the increased demand for labour and the increased demand for credit squeeze profits and incentivize capitalists to try to 'innovate their way out of a crisis', which is facilitated by the credit system. Ultimately, an event that undermines confidence triggers the crash and causes people to re-evaluate the value of credit monies. When it becomes apparent that credit monies cannot be serviced by future surplus-value creation,

> The devaluation of capital, and of the labourer, proceed apace. Capitalists seek to stay alive by cannibalizing upon each other. The labourer is likewise sacrificed on the altar of the underlying irrationality of capitalism. Crisis, as the irrational rationalizer of the economic system, cuts a grim swathe across the economic landscape of capitalist society. (Ibid.: 305)

It can therefore be shown that the codependence of capital and labour is progressively antagonistic under conditions of competition and in light of the prevalence of the tendency to engage in accumulation for accumulation's sake, because capital serves to progressively undermine the basis of its own existence – labour.

As Holloway (1992: 159) notes, crisis can be understood as expressions of 'the structural instability of capitalist social relations'. However, whereas Joseph Schumpeter (2010 [1943]: 73) suggested that capitalism 'incessantly revolutionizes the economic structure *from within*, incessantly destroying the old one, incessantly creating a new one' in a process of 'creative destruction', Marxist theory views crisis differently. While it acknowledges that 'crisis is both breakdown and restructuring, both instability and restabilisation of class relations', which can restructure capital and provide conditions for accumulation to begin anew (Holloway 1992: 164), that is not the *purpose* of crisis. To make this connection is to argue that the tendency towards crisis is a tendency to reproduce capitalist social relations on a new footing, and suggests that no alternative to capitalism is possible. Rather, these crisis tendencies contain the potential for rupture, in which 'conflict becomes manifest, the "normal" is questioned, other views of this normality gain force, hidden interconnections appear, established patterns of power are attacked' (ibid.: 165). In the inherent crisis tendencies of capitalist social relations, therefore, lies not only a rationale for an alternative to capitalism, but also the kernels of its creation.

The suggestion that capitalism is inherently crisis-prone is appealing simply in light of the repeated occurrences of crises in capitalism throughout history. However, it also presents a theoretical conception of why this occurs that is rooted in the way in which value is created, and can account both for periods of apparent relative prosperity like those seen in the 1920s, 1960s and 1990s, as well as the speculative financial activity that sustained the booms and ultimately collapsed in the 1930s, 1970s and 2000s. In being able to convincingly account for the apparent tendency towards crisis in theory, and in a way that can help us explain the specific dynamic of historical instances of crisis of capitalism, it also offers the basis of a theory of stability by establishing a rationale for an alternative to capitalism, in which social relations are not progressively antagonistic in the context of competition and the tendency to engage in accumulation for accumulation's sake.

Conclusions

The chapter has argued that the relationships between state and economy suggested by the political economy of Adam Smith, John Maynard Keynes and Friedrich Hayek have each been realized in historical context in the periods of laissez-faire liberalism, the era of embedded liberalism and the era of neoliberalism, respectively. However, it has also shown how the relationships between the state and the economy that prevailed in these periods were unable to prevent the interwar collapse and the Great Depression, the break-up of Bretton Woods and the 1970s stagflation, or the sub-prime mortgage crisis and the Great Recession. The chapter therefore argued that there are inherent crisis tendencies in capitalism that stem from the contradictions in the codependence of labour and capital in the context of competition, and the tendency to engage in accumulation for accumulation's sake.

The repeated occurrences of crises in capitalism surveyed here, and the identification of a clear crisis dynamic within capitalism, provide a powerful rationale for an alternative to capitalism; if the injustices and contradictions of capitalism are fundamental pathologies, then attempting to address them within the framework of the existing system represents little more than sticking plaster. In order to address the injustices and contradictions that stem from capitalism itself, changes in the essence of that system are needed so that history need not repeat itself. Pursuing wealth for its own sake, history and theoretical reflection tell us, simply does not work, and the costs in terms of poverty and social injustice are great. In light of the pervasive nature of capitalism and its far-reaching grasp, it is tempting to suggest that, regardless of this fact, there is nothing that can be done. We might ask, how can such an apparently monolithic set of structures and institutions be overcome and replaced with something new and untested without fundamentally compromising our ability to meet our basic needs, and without succumbing to resistance from that system itself? However, as the previous chapter argued, the world we live in has no existence separate from our social action; it takes its form from the way in which people interact with one another, and the way in which people interact with one another depends on the ideas we have about capitalism and its consequences. This chapter has argued that capitalism is not only prone to crises, but that crisis is hard-wired into its very fabric. If future crises, and the social consequences that come with them, are to be avoided, an alternative is the only option.

3 | ALTERNATIVES TO CAPITALISM

Introduction

The previous two chapters have shown two things. First, it has been shown that the way in which wealth is created, distributed and exchanged in capitalism has been understood in different ways. In turn, this has implications for how we understand the problem of stability and crisis in capitalism. Secondly, it has been demonstated that capitalist social relations have shown a historical tendency towards crisis. This manifested itself in events such as the Great Depression, the 1970s stagflation and the Great Recession. While each of the understandings of capitalism has its own understanding of where crisis comes from, this book has argued that capitalism itself is an *inherently* crisis-prone system because of the nature of its competitive dynamics and the exploitation of working people inherent in these competitive dynamics.

Furthermore, this book has argued that crises have been addressed through working-class subsidy of capitalists who have engaged in accumulation for accumulation's sake and whose capitals must be devalued, which means workers suffer doubly from the precariousness of their employment position and cuts to welfare provision that are imposed as states seek to finance the costs of crisis through the politics of austerity. On the basis of its discussion of crisis dynamics in capitalism, the book has established a rationale for an alternative form of production, distribution and exchange – an alternative (to) capitalism. The purpose of this chapter is to discuss three such alternatives and their implications.

The first section of the chapter considers an alternative capitalism rather than an alternative *to* capitalism, which returns to liberal ideas. Extrapolating from the ideas of Hayek, who believed state intervention distorted markets, the section considers whether a radically minimal (yet strong) state in the libertarian tradition is able to account for crises in capitalism and provide a stable alternative. The second section of the chapter considers an alternative to capitalism in the form of a cooperative economy, which incorporates social and civil objectives alongside pecuniary gain as primary objectives. On the basis of the same rationale, the final section of the chapter considers the merits of an alternative to capitalism in the form of a socialist economy, in which the means of production are taken into public ownership for the benefit of all.

The chapter argues that the alternative capitalism and the two alternatives to capitalism discussed all have weaknesses that make it necessary for us to think of an alternative (to) capitalism as a *process* that must be continually made and remade, rather than as an *outcome* or *utopia*. The chapter will ultimately suggest that the libertarian alternative capitalism relies on fundamental assumptions about the nature of private property that mean its theoretical foundations can be questioned, and that even if these foundations were sustainable, the position would ultimately be incompatible with social stability because of the tendency towards inequality inherent within it. However, it also identifies problems with the cooperative and socialist forms of organization, in their respective tendencies towards degeneration and the reproduction of particular inequalities of capitalism respectively. The purpose of the chapter is to argue that there is no 'correct' alternative (to) capitalism, but that the creation of a post-capitalist future relies on the maintenance of pluralism, diversity and experimentation.

A libertarian alternative capitalism

Chapter 1 showed how Adam Smith rejected the notion that wealth was to be found in the stock of precious metals, but rather stemmed from the productive capacity of nations derived from the division of labour. This, he argued, was a natural characteristic of humankind, as each person acting according to his or her own self-interest would promote the good of society more broadly conceived. This was possible because people acting in their self-interest is not the same as them acting selfishly – people, he had argued, were able to sympathize with the situation of others in their community and make judgements about their own actions with this in mind. Smith also believed that wealth was distributed among society according to the varying contributions that land, labour and capital made to its creation. As such, there was no a priori case for the redistribution of incomes and wealth, the extensive intervention of the state in the economy, or reform to the democratic institutions of the state to directly incorporate the interests of a broader franchise.

Friedrich Hayek continued in this tradition with his belief that the price mechanism was the most efficient mode of transmitting relevant information to market actors. In this way, it would be possible for market economies to reach a stable equilibrium even though no individual or group of individuals had planned for this to occur. He believed that any intervention from the state in planning the economy or in distributing resources would lead to a suboptimal outcome as incentives and patterns of distribution would be distorted. It is the protection of private property then, which should form the principal function of the state. As a result of his belief that the restoration of markets to profitability through the reduction of wages and unemployment was absolutely necessary, some commentators 'admired Hayek's realism about how capitalism worked, but thought him politically naïve: such a policy, if pursued, would lose capitalism all political legitimacy' (Gamble 1996a: 46).

Understanding the origin of crisis in the liberal tradition therefore begins by assuming that capitalism is not crisis-prone as such, but tends towards crisis only when the market is distorted by external intervention. The cause of crises is not states' failure to plan for competition. The solution to crisis, therefore, lies not in the extension of regulation, but in the retreat of such market-distorting actions; states should retreat to a position in which they facilitate and police the market but no more. Similarly, they should retreat to a position where they protect individuals in society from harm, but have no duty to provide for them. In fact, providing for people beyond a certain limit has the potential to introduce just the kind of distortion into the price mechanism that the liberal tradition believed would produce suboptimal outcomes and ultimately result in crisis. From this position, it is possible to establish a rationale in the liberal tradition for an alternative form of capitalism that involves a further retreat of the state from public provision, and a strengthening of its role in the protection of individual freedom – in particular people's freedom to own private property – so that the market may operate most efficiently.

In addition to the apparent benefits of such a minimal state that can be extrapolated from neoliberal thought in political economy, Robert Nozick has argued that such a minimal form of the state – the libertarian form of the state – is the only form of the state that can be justified on the grounds of social justice. 'Individuals have rights', Nozick (1974: ix) begins, 'and there are things no person or group may do to them (without violating their rights).' This means that it is absolutely essential for us to consider, in our discussion of a stable and just form of social organization that meets people's needs by providing for the production, distribution and exchange of the goods and services that they require, 'the question of what, if anything, the state and its officials may do. How much room do individual rights leave for the state?' Going beyond Smith, Hayek and the liberal tradition, Nozick argues that not only is a minimal (strong) state required, it is the only state compatible with principles of social justice:

a minimal state, limited to the narrow functions of protection against force, theft, fraud, enforcement of contracts, and so on, is justified; [...] any more extensive state will violate persons' rights not to be forced to do certain things, and is unjustified; [...] the minimal state is inspiring as well as right. Two noteworthy implications are that the state may not use its coercive apparatus for the purpose of getting some citizens to aid others, or in order to prohibit activities to people for their *own* good or protection. (Ibid.: ix)

The basis of the libertarian position is therefore the right to self-ownership. From a political economy perspective, liberals argue that markets are efficient; from a social philosophy perspective, they argue that they are also just. Going beyond Hayek's idea that the intervention of the state should be avoided because it is inefficient, libertarianism argues that it is also fair: 'There is no *central* distribution, no person *entitled* to control all the resources, jointly deciding how they are to be doled out' (ibid.: 149; first emphasis in the original, second added). Nozick's theory is therefore one of entitlement, as he imagines a society in which outcomes are 'the product of many individual decisions which the different individuals are entitled to make' (ibid.: 150).

Justice involves a consideration of three things. Namely, how property comes to be owned in the first instance, how it is subsequently transferred, and how past injustices in the acquisition and transfer of property should be rectified (ibid.: 151–2). Justice, then, should not prescribe any kind of distribution that is just; justice is a historical matter that is determined not only by the way things are as they stand and how they might be in the future, but also by how the present state of affairs came about. If the present state of affairs came about according to the principles of justice in acquisition and transfer, then that distribution is just (ibid.: 153–4). Nozick (ibid.: 160) provides us with the following maxim that enshrines his theory of justice: '*From each as they choose, to each as they are chosen*'.

The libertarian position therefore represents an alternative form of capitalism that could be justified on the basis of two claims. First, the state's retreat to act only in order to protect people's right of self-ownership would reduce distortions in the transfer of information via the price mechanism, and therefore contribute to economic stability. Secondly, while this might result in inequalities between people in terms of the distribution of resources, there can be no normative objection to this on the grounds of social justice so long as the original acquisition of goods and their subsequent transfer were conducted according to robust principles of justice. However, Nozick argues that not only is the position justifiable, it is also inevitable. In order to make this point, he asks us to imagine a distribution (D1) that you believe to be just; 'perhaps everyone has an equal share, perhaps shares vary in accordance with some dimension you treasure'. He then asks us to imagine that a sports star in great demand (in his example, the basketball player Wilt Chamberlain) signs a contract to play for a team in which a certain percentage of gate receipts goes straight to them. People willingly pay this percentage of their admission into a separate pot with the sports star's name on it. At the end of the season, the sports star ends up with a much greater share than others and we have a new distribution (D2) in which there is an inequality between most members of society and the sports star. 'If D1 was a just distribution', Nozick (ibid.: 161) asks, 'and people voluntarily moved from it to D2, transferring parts of their shares they were given under D1 (what was it for if not to do something with?), isn't D2 also just?' On the basis that each person will have their own consumption preferences that will not be met under an original distribution, D1, trade will be required. It logically follows, then, that no distribution that prescribes what people should possess rather than providing a framework for what they are entitled to 'can be continuously realized without continuous intervention in people's lives' that would violate their self-ownership (ibid.: 163).

According to liberal political economy, it is interventions like this which are also the source of the inefficiencies that lead to undesirable outcomes. The libertarian position supplements this claim with the claim that the minimal state protecting only freedom and private property is also a just system. The strength of this libertarian claim is fundamentally dependent upon how we perceive of the initial acquisition of property. In order to make the libertarian case for justice on this basis, Nozick's entitlement theory draws on the work of John Locke (1764 [1689]: 216–17), who argued that:

> Though the earth and all inferior creatures be common to all men, yet every man has a *property* in his own *person* [...] Whatsoever, then, he removes out of the state that Nature hath provided, and left it in, he hath mixed his *labour* with, and joined to it something that is his own, and thereby makes it his *property* [...] For this *labour* being the unquestionable property of the labourer, no man but he can have a right to what that is once joined to, at least where there is enough, and as good left in common for others.

From this we can distil some important claims. First, everybody owns their own labour-power. Secondly, mixing labour with natural resources gives a legitimate title to ownership. Thirdly, such appropriations of property can be justified as long as opportunities for others to do the same are not removed (see Day 1966; Drury 1982).

For contemporary liberals, this justification for private property ownership has been interpreted as meaning simply that the acquisition of property must not make other people 'worse off by being unable to use what they previously could' (Drury 1982: 29). Property is seen as a natural right so long as appropriation by any individual does not waste something that might be used by somebody else. However, it was not Locke's intention to claim that there are only natural limits to the acquisition of property. Drury (ibid.: 32) explains how Locke intended his 'enough and as good' proviso to apply only to 'the first ages of the world', where 'Just as it is not possible for anyone to drink a river dry, so it is not possible for anyone to acquire possessions through labour that would prejudice the position of others.' Rather, in a more advanced society, a moral imperative takes over, in which the natural right to appropriation on the grounds of self-preservation is subsumed to social preservation because in the first ages of the world the 'right to property did not threaten the right to life, but ensured it' (ibid.: 34) because the system of private property 'encourages labour and industry, and this in turn [...] improves the standard of living of everyone in society' (ibid.: 35).

This weaker approach to the Lockean proviso on property acquisition is the one that Nozick subscribes to. While he raises several questions about the plausibility of the argument that mixing one's labour with a previously unowned property represents a just acquisition, in a similar vein to Locke, he does suggest that 'A process normally giving rise to a permanent bequeathable property right in a previously unowned thing will not do so if the position of others no longer at liberty to use the thing is thereby worsened' (Nozick 1974: 178). He notes how this also implies that where the original acquisition of the total supply of some good would be unjust, the subsequent purchase of a total supply of that good would also be unjust, although never likely to occur since the difficulty in acquiring the remaining supply increases as stock diminishes (ibid.: 179). In the event that there is a fundamental change in circumstances that leaves one owner of a certain good with the total usable supply of it, Nozick (ibid.: 180) suggests that their individual right to do what they will with this property is 'overridden to avoid some catastrophe'.

While appearing strong, the claim that the libertarian alternative capitalism is just can be challenged on the basis of a distinction between unowned and commonly owned property. For Nozick, all land is originally unowned, rather than owned jointly, or owned in common. However, 'Why', G. A. Cohen (1985: 91) asks, was property's 'original privatization not a theft of what rightly should be held in common?' It is 'relevantly false', he suggested, that all things have entitlements over them when they are created because 'all external private property either is, or was made of, something which was once no one's private property, either in fact or morally [...] In the prehistory of any existing piece of private property there was at least one moment at which something privately unowned was taken into private ownership' (ibid.: 91–2). If we question the assumption that land is originally unowned, and suggest instead that it is jointly or collectively owned, Cohen (ibid.: 98) argues that 'the proper way to decide its fate would be by the socialist device of consensual agreement, instead of unilaterally', as Nozick claims. Furthermore, there is no reason to suggest that this was not the true state of affairs, and that 'if joint ownership rather than no-ownership is, morally speaking, the original position, then [one person] has the right to forbid [another person] to appropriate, even if [the first person] would benefit from what [they] thereby forbid' (ibid.: 99). The moral foundation on which Nozick's entitlement theory of private property is based, and which justifies the strong but minimal state on normative grounds, is therefore built upon a questionable assumption.

Not only does Cohen note that Nozick's premise, upon which his theory of entitlement is based, is controversial, he also suggests he is inconsistent. This is because Nozick argues that it is unjust for a policy to be introduced against somebody's wishes, even if it benefits them as an unintended consequence, but allows for the introduction of policy against somebody's will if it benefits them as intended (ibid.: 103). This can be seen in the sense that he regards taxation in all of its forms (whether it benefits an individual directly or not) as a violation of property rights, but allows one individual to appropriate property against the will of another person, as long as the second person does not lose out from the appropriation (ibid.: 103). 'Therefore', Cohen (ibid.: 104) argues, 'Nozick cannot claim to be inspired throughout by a desire to protect freedom, unless he means by "freedom" what he really does mean by it: the freedom of private property-owners to do as they wish with their property.' In this formulation, Cohen (1985, 1986) suggests that the self-ownership of some people (property owners) is privileged over the self-ownership of others (the property-less).

Extrapolating from neoliberal understandings of economic crisis, the libertarian position suggests that this form of organization would be stable. However, in the context of the inequality that appears to be an inevitable consequence of libertarianism, this seems questionable. This is because the transfer of wealth from a large group of people to a smaller group of people means the majority will have progressively less income to spend on the goods and services that they need. The reduction in the demand for goods and services would also be likely to increase unemployment when industries cease to be profitable, and therefore further exacerbate social tension caused by inequality. Were it the case that all consumption decisions were like Nozick's Wilt Chamberlain example – the consumption of luxury goods – this would not be problematic in the sense that people would be able to adjust their preferences and decide not to consume certain goods. The only consequence would be a corresponding drop in Wilt Chamberlain's income. However, it is clearly not the case that all consumption decisions can be forgone or substituted, as people need to buy the very things that they need to survive such as food, clothing and shelter. If this also involves the continued redistribution of wealth to those who have property from those who do not, it is not clear that such a situation would be sustainable because the property-less would find themselves increasingly impoverished in relative terms, regardless of whether or not there was justice in the original acquisition of property and its subsequent transfer. The extent to which people will continue to accept large-scale relative inequalities in incomes and wealth is clearly open to question, but historical revolutionary experience suggests that this encounters definite limits.

These criticisms of libertarianism therefore raise important questions about the possibility of incorporating an egalitarian element into a libertarian alternative capitalism. Michael Otsuka (2003: 3) has addressed this question and suggested that 'a robust right of self-ownership is, across a fairly wide range of individuals who differ in their capabilities, perfectly compatible with a highly egalitarian principle which calls for a distribution of worldly resources which equalizes opportunity for welfare'. Otsuka does this by maintaining a strong conception of self-ownership that prohibits forced labour and endorses an individual's right to the whole fruits of their labour (ibid.: 15), and critiquing Nozick's claim that taxation is equivalent to forced labour. He argues that if it could be shown that taxation is not always equivalent to forced labour, then taxation would be perfectly compatible with the strong right to self-ownership that libertarians advocate.

One such case where taxation would be acceptable is a luxury tax, in which payments would be required only after those liable had acquired an abundance of material resources. In this situation, taxation would have no meaningful bearing on the existence of those liable, which also means it would be easy to avoid: those who would become liable to pay such a tax could simply stop producing before they reach the threshold of liability. In this scenario, taxation could not represent 'forced labour, since it would be so easy to avoid' (ibid.: 18). What Otsuka presents us with, then, is a conception of libertarian thought that perceives redistribution not as a violation of the right of self-ownership, but as a violation of property rights (ibid.: 19). How, then, can the alternative libertarian form of social and economic organization be reconciled with egalitarian principles in a way that can counter objections raised on the basis of social instability that stems from inequality?

The problem for Nozick's version of libertarianism, according to Otsuka (ibid.: 20), is his claim that 'one's right of ownership over worldly resources that one uses in order to earn income is as full as one's right of ownership over oneself'. Otsuka (ibid.: 23) rejects this position on the basis that it allows the first acquirers of private property to make their acquisitions as long as they pay others a wage that leaves them no worse off than they would be under a state of nature. Not only does this leave those who are not the first to acquire land to an existence dependent on wage labour, Nozick's position allows for 'first-grabbing' acquisitions of land, 'even when chances [for first-grabbing] are not equal' (ibid.: 23).

A revised right of acquisition therefore suggests that 'You may acquire previously unowned worldly resources if and only if you leave enough so that everyone else can acquire an equally advantageous share of unowned worldly resources' (ibid.: 24). While the meaning of the proviso is open to interpretation, Otsuka (ibid.: 25) takes it to mean that everybody is able to achieve 'the same level of welfare as anybody else given the combination of her worldly and personal resources'. Under conditions where those who have possession of natural resources have no desire to produce goods above those needed for their own subsistence, this egalitarian proviso would not be consistent with the robust libertarian emphasis on self-ownership, because equality could be achieved only by limiting people's right of acquisition. However, if those who were more able could acquire a sufficient proportion of worldly resources to produce goods and services beyond levels needed for their own subsistence, the less able 'would be able to support themselves through truly voluntary exchanges with the able-bodied that did not involve forced assistance' (ibid.: 33):

> To provide a simple and artificial illustration of such an arrangement, imagine an island society divided into a large number of able-bodied and a smaller number of disabled individuals. All the sea-front property is divided among the disabled, and farmable land in the interior is divided among the able-bodied. The able-bodied each voluntarily purchase access to the beach in exchange for the provision of food to the disabled. The result of this division of land is that the disabled and the able-bodied are each able to better themselves to an equal degree without anyone's being forced to come to the assistance of anybody else. (Ibid.: 33)

So far, then, libertarianism can lay claim to being a more desirable alternative form of social and economic organization to the prevailing form of actually existing capitalism on the grounds that less interference from the state will allow markets to operate efficiently, that it will protect individuals' incontrovertible rights to self-ownership, and that this is compatible, in principle, with an egalitarian conception of social justice.

The principal problem with Otsuka's position in terms of developing an alternative form of capitalism is its abstract basis, which the author himself acknowledges. The scenarios imagined fundamentally depend on a very particular distribution of worldly resources among particular groups. In reality, the distribution of arable land in the interior and seafront properties is unevenly distributed between the able-bodied and the disabled, and would be even if Otsuka's egalitarian proviso for property acquisition were adhered to. This presents individuals with the right of self-ownership to trade access to the seafront with the products of arable land with the able-bodied *or* the disabled. Even if property were distributed between the able-bodied and disabled as Otsuka imagines in his theoretical construction, it is clear that some seafront land would be more desirable and attract more visitors than others. This is problematic because in such scenarios there can be no guarantee that people will exercise their right to self-ownership in a way that will produce sufficiency of welfare. Resources may be transferred from the able-bodied to the able-bodied at the expense of the disabled, or from the able-bodied to particular disabled people and not others. Unless property acquisition is determined by a particular pre-distribution that means the able-bodied must trade with the disabled (or particular disabled people) in order to meet their welfare needs, the problem of inequality and therefore social instability re-emerges. However, if such a pre-distribution existed, it is clear that there would be infringements of the libertarian principle of self-ownership on which the position rests, and that it would be anathema to liberal political economists' objections to planning. While such a critique of Otsuka is in some respects unfair, since it is his intention to show the logical possibility of an egalitarian libertarianism rather than to develop a programme for realizing it, it remains the case that in anything other than the abstract, the case for a libertarian egalitarian alternative capitalism appears to collapse back into itself.

This section of the chapter departed from the liberal position that crises stem from interference in the transfer of relevant information through the price system, and that they can therefore be avoided by minimizing such interferences through a further retreat of the state from intervention in markets and the provision of welfare. It therefore presented libertarianism as a form of social organization that represents an alternative capitalism, and showed how various libertarian thinkers have attempted to demonstrate its desirability in terms of social justice on the basis of arguments about the right to self-ownership and the acquisition of property. Ultimately, this section of the chapter has concluded that questions can be raised about such a position in terms of the implications that inequality is likely to have for social stability if moves towards a libertarian form of organization were realized. It has also suggested that attempts to reconcile libertarianism and equality might appear strong in the abstract sense, but are unlikely to be able to produce the outcomes they envisage in practice without forgoing at least some of the rights that are seen to be immutable by libertarians. As such, this examination of a libertarian alternative capitalism suggests that it is likely to create similar kinds of tensions to those we have seen under the neoliberal state form, and not resolve them by reducing distortions that disrupt the efficient operation of markets.

A cooperative alternative to capitalism

In Chapter 1 we saw how Marx believed that the way in which wealth was created under capitalist social relations is fundamentally dependent on the exploitation of one class of people by another. Under these conditions, those in possession of the means of production are able to pay those who have nothing to sell but their labour-power less than the value of the commodities they create, and keep the surplus for themselves. It was also shown in Chapter 1 how the competitive logic of capitalism acted to drive down wages and replace living labour with machinery, contributing to the impoverishment of the working classes. Chapter 2 then linked this competitive logic and the impoverishment of workers to the evolution of crises in capitalism, and suggested that as a result of these dynamics capitalist social relations should be viewed as being in a constant state of crisis.

This provides a rationale for another kind of alternative to the prevailing form of capitalism, in which competition and the quest for profit are not the primary driving forces of social and economic relations. In principle, this would have the potential to mute the crisis dynamic Marx envisaged in capitalist social relations, and in the process alleviate the exploitation on which capitalism depends for the expansion of value. For one group of eighteenth-century socialists, sometimes called utopian socialists, typified by the writings of Robert Owen, this could be achieved through cooperative (or mutual) association in which production, distribution and exchange would be organized with civic and social goals in mind as well as pecuniary gain. In Marxian terminology, a far greater emphasis would be placed on the creation of use-values than under the prevailing capitalist form of organization.

Robert Heilbroner (2000: 107) described the cooperative community that Robert Owen founded at New Lanark in Scotland as 'one spot in Britain [that] shone like a beacon through the storm' of the Industrial Revolution. In the community at New Lanark, standards of living were much higher than in the large industrial towns elsewhere in Britain; there were 'neat rows of workers' homes with *two* rooms in every house; here were streets with the garbage neatly piled up awaiting disposal' (ibid.: 107). Young children did not work in the factories, but 'Instead of running wild and fierce through the streets, they were found by the visitors to be fast at work and play in a large school house' (ibid.: 108). Following from these early endeavours of cooperative association, it is possible to see an alternative to capitalism established over 150 years ago that survives in the form of the contemporary cooperative movement.

Like Marxist analysis, utopian socialism stems from a critique of the prevailing form of social and economic organization (Goodwin 1978: 13); as Robert Owen wrote in the preface to his second essay in *A New View of Society*, 'It is [...] an important step gained when the cause of evil is ascertained. The next is to devise a remedy for the evil, which shall create the least possible inconvenience' (Owen 1991: 3). On the first matter, Owen (ibid.: 94) observed that the rise of manufacturing had led to vast increases in wealth and influence for Britain, but brought with it 'accompanying evils of such a magnitude as to raise a doubt whether the latter do not preponderate over the former', and it is worth quoting Owen's opinions about the relationship between the accumulation of wealth and the well-being of people at length:

> The acquisition of wealth, and the desire which it naturally creates for a continued increase, have introduced a fondness

for essentially injurious luxuries among a numerous class of individuals who formerly never thought of them, and they have also generated a disposition which strongly impels its possessors to sacrifice the best feelings of human nature to this love of accumulation. (Ibid.: 95)

Moreover, this state of affairs was specifically capitalistic, and had

been carried by new competitors striving against those of longer standing, to a point of real oppression, reducing [working people] by successive changes, as the spirit of competition increased and the ease of acquiring wealth diminished, to a state more wretched than can be imagined by those who have not attentively observed changes as they have gradually occurred. (Ibid.: 95)

As an industrialist in the textile industry himself, he was perhaps an unlikely advocate of reform; however, he was ardent in his belief that the competitive logic of capitalism was unjust and inefficient. As it was widely acknowledged that paying sufficient care to ensure machinery was well kept and in good order produced productive gains, Owen asked of his fellow capitalists, 'If, then, due care as to the state of your inanimate machines can produce such beneficial results, what may not be expected if you devote equal attention to your vital machines, which are far more wonderfully constructed?' (ibid.: 5). Owen therefore rejected the subordination of human labour to the newly introduced machinery and based his programme of social reform around the principle that the interests, welfare and well-being of people should be treated as seriously as profit-seeking. In so doing, Owen argued that it would not only be possible to increase the well-being of people more broadly, but that it would also be in the interests of the capitalists themselves.

Owen was not simply an advocate of such actions, but also put them into practice. To aid recruitment for the mills at New Lanark, Owen's predecessor had built residences and made them available at a low rent, and care was provided for children. However, this succeeded only in attracting small numbers of 'ragged labourers', and many children continued to work long hours before receiving any education in the evenings. This meant that many young people left the community at the end of their apprenticeships (Sargant 2005 [1860]: 31–2). As a result, Owen believed that more thorough reform had to be undertaken. This began with Owen's provision of high-quality goods in the shops at New Lanark, which were sold at cost price, and 'by giving [people] a part to play in the government of the village' (ibid.: 37). This involved the participation of members of the community in reaching judgements about cases of misconduct (ibid.: 37; Harrison 1969: 158); however, the primary means by which social behaviour would be encouraged was through *'The Silent Monitor.* This consisted of a four-sided piece of wood, about two inches long and one broad; with the sides painted respectively, black, white, yellow, and blue' (Sargant 2005 [1860]: 38), which was hung at the workplace of each person. The colour at the front 'denoted the conduct of the worker during the previous day' (Harrison 1969: 158). The sale of alcoholic beverages in the villages was restricted and fines were levied for misdemeanours (ibid.: 158).

Heilbroner (2000: 108) noted how *The Silent Monitor* mainly indicated good character on the part of the workers at New Lanark, and J. C. F. Harrison (1969: 158–9, fn 4) has shown how a variety of indicators were taken as an indication that the philosophy of New Lanark produced positive social results; the recording of only twenty-eight illegitimate births in the period 1810–19, for instance, was taken as a sign that 'the moral habits of the people are … very exemplary'; 'The schools at New Lanark', he furthermore observed, 'drew more encomiums from reformers than any other aspect of the great experiment' (ibid.: 160). In light of these apparent successes, the New Lanark experiment spawned at least sixteen communities in its image in the United States, catalysed by Owen's investment in New Harmony, and a further seven in the United Kingdom (ibid.: 163).

However, as the communities were formed they were increasingly beset by problems. In various cases there was a dislike of Owen's religious views and tension over communal property arrangements. For instance, some people found that a communal existence did not suit them; this was the reason that the American novelist Nathaniel Hawthorne decided not to persevere with his participation in the Brook Farm experiment. On this matter, he wrote:

I am troubled with many doubts (after my experience last year) whether I, as an individual, am a proper subject for these beneficial influences. In an economical point of view, undoubtedly, I would not do so well anywhere else; but I feel that this ought not to be the primary consideration. A more important question is, how my intellectual and moral condition, and my ability to be useful, would be affected by merging myself in a community. I confess to you, my dear Sir, it is my present belief that I can best attain the higher ends of my life by retaining the ordinary relation to society. (Hawthorne 1939: 730)

In other cases, the financial burden of communities became too great to bear, especially in instances where there was the withdrawal or death of a major benefactor (see Harrison 1969: 163–75). While New Lanark had produced some general benefits for the community, the record of other cooperative experiments does not read as well. Hardly any had longevity beyond a few years, and 'most of them were plagued by internal strife, and their impact upon society at large appears to have been negligible' (ibid.: 175). In America at least, the intention of new communities was not to develop 'the new moral world' that Owen had envisaged, but to deal with shortages in capital, expertise and institutions that were typical of American frontier life (ibid.: 177). The communities also attracted 'persons who were in some ways social misfits [as] Community was a solution to problems of personal deficiency or social maladjustment, and had an obvious appeal to those who sought security or escape from the world' (ibid.: 179).

The utopian socialists, typified by the ideas of Robert Owen, therefore had a robust critique of the prevailing industrial society in the nineteenth century and sought to address those ills through the construction of societies that operated on the basis of mutuality and cooperation rather than individualism and competition. By providing opportunities for education and access to good-quality housing, healthcare and clothing, Owen believed that people could be encouraged to work together for a social benefit. In other words, by retreating from the competitive logic of capitalism, the pernicious effects of that system could be avoided. In combination and working with one another, the utopian socialists believed that a more prosperous society could be formed. However, in light of the failure of the nineteenth-century cooperative communities, the question remains whether the ideas of the utopian socialists represent a plausible and/ or desirable alternative to capitalism.

Barbara Goodwin (1978: 30) has described Owen's propositions about the rationality of human beings and the potential for moral character to be developed as principles 'adopted without proof [...] believing that such facts would gain general credence through assertion alone'; Heilbroner (2000: 125) described the utopian socialists as 'reformers of the heart rather than the head', and a contemporary biographer of Robert Owen prefaced his work by suggesting that 'If [Owen] had died in middle life, before he had earned the antipathy of society by the loud proclamation of his ill-considered moral philosophy [...] his memory would have been revered' (Sargant 2005 [1860]: xxi).

These presentations of the mutual ideas of the utopian socialists are representative of broader views of other factions of socialists. Lenin (1913: 4) praised the utopians for their criticism of society and the fact that it 'condemned and damned it [...] dreamed of its destruction [...] had visions of a better order and endeavoured to convince the rich of the immorality of exploitation'. However, he was equally critical in the next stroke of his pen, arguing that 'utopian socialism did not indicate the real solution [...] it could not reveal the laws of capitalist development, or show what social force is capable of becoming a new creator of society' (ibid.: 4). However, others, in particular Marx and Engels, developed a critique of this nature much further.

Marx and Engels (1985 [1848]: 116) also noted how the utopian socialists 'attack every principle of existing society' and as a result 'are full of the most valuable materials for the enlightenment of the working class'. However, while Engels appears to have had some interest in the experimental communities of the utopian socialists, from an early stage Marx was sceptical about the value of such endeavours and Engels later came around to this view (Leopold 2005: 445). Engels (1908: 59) in particular noted how the views of the utopian socialists were formed at a time when capitalism was at an early stage of development, meaning as a result that their blueprints for a mutually organized cooperative future could not be successful. 'To the crude conditions of capitalistic productions and the crude class conditions', Engels wrote, 'corresponded crude theories [...] the more completely they were worked out in detail, the more they could not avoid drifting off into pure phantasies.' The weakness of utopian socialism for Marx and Engels therefore lay in the utopian socialists' idealistic conception of history, which neglected the class struggle. In *The Communist Manifesto*, Marx and Engels (1985 [1848]: 114–18) criticize the utopian movement for its philanthropic base and particularly the notion that the working classes can be freed from their oppression through the goodwill and the example of the upper classes. As a corollary of this, they criticize the utopians for their rejection of 'all political, and especially all revolutionary action'. The book will return to these issues in Chapter 4.

It seems that the fate of mutual experiments in Britain and America, and their critical reception by other socialists, might suggest that cooperative and mutual organization is not a desirable alternative to capitalism either in principle or in practice. However, it is important to note that the criticisms of Marx and Engels were carefully qualified. As David Leopold (2005: 452) has noted, 'they are usually relatively generous about the original utopians and comparatively critical of their successors and subsequent imitators'. This is because the first generation of utopians were writing at a time when it was not possible for them to fully understand the dynamics of the class struggle. The same cannot be said for their successors, who had a greater opportunity to develop this understanding from historical experience. As Marx and Engels (1985 [1848]: 117) wrote, 'although the originators of these systems were, in many respects, revolutionary, their disciples have, in every case, formed mere reactionary sects'. Leopold (2005: 461) offers a useful analogy by comparing the difference between 'utopian' and 'scientific' socialism with the difference between alchemy and chemistry: 'Chemists (and scientific socialists) should honour their alchemic (and utopian) predecessors (without, of course, repeating their mistakes).'

However, the theoretical critique of utopian socialism does not completely undermine the case for cooperative organization as an alternative to capitalism. While many observers, with the benefit of hindsight, saw the collapse of early cooperative communities as inevitable, cooperative forms of organization have continued to operate alongside the capitalist economy since the Rochdale Pioneers formed their cooperative movement in 1844 (Heilbroner 2000: 114). As Erik Olin Wright (2010: 236) observes, 'Workers' co-ops have continued through the subsequent history of capitalist development, although today, with a few notable exceptions, they are mostly relatively small, local operations.' One of these notable exceptions is the Mondragón cooperatives in the Basque region of northern Spain, which were formed in 1956 as a single producer of paraffin heaters and later expanded with the formation of a cooperative bank and a coordinating institution for other cooperatives in the area (ibid.: 240). This was followed by governance reforms in the early 1990s, which formed the Mondragón Cooperative Corporation and aimed to make 'a more efficient system of governance and coordination that would enable the complex of cooperatives to compete more effectively in markets outside of the Basque region itself' (ibid.: 241). By making contributions to the Mondragón Cooperative Corporation, individual cooperatives strengthen the system's infrastructure, which not only aims at preserving the cooperative organization, but also expanding it (ibid.: 241).

The motives for participation in cooperative endeavours in contemporary society are somewhat different from those envisaged by Owen and the utopian socialists. While the utopians envisaged a wholesale reform of society, contemporary workers' cooperatives are more often viewed as a means of giving people control over their own work lives and therefore reducing alienation and exploitation, while contemporary consumers' cooperatives are able to offer people the opportunity to make consumption decisions on the basis of judgements about ethics and sustainability. Neil Carter (2006: 416–17), for instance, has noted that workers' cooperatives are set up for reasons that include people's social and political ambitions, and their discontent with or rejection of 'the conventional bureaucratic organisation structures of the capitalist firm'. However, he nonetheless questions the plausibility of the idea that cooperative organization, a priori, can reduce alienation: 'Whether working in a democratic or authoritarian workplace,' he notes, 'boring work is boring work' (ibid.: 420).

Janelle Cornwell (2012: 730), in contrast, found during three years of ethnographic research involving a worker cooperative in Massachusetts called Collective Copies that it was not simply the nature of the work undertaken which contributed to workers' well-being. Even where people had moved into the cooperative from similar capitalist firms elsewhere, and were carrying out similar tasks, the recognition by fellow members of the importance of a personal and social life in the cooperative were seen as a very important goal of the enterprise. Whereas Cornwell (ibid.: 730) found that one employee had been made redundant from a capitalist competitor for picking up a sick child from school, Collective Copies gave members a great deal of control over shift scheduling as well as providing flexibility at moments of crisis. Through compromise and cooperation, this approach to time management was successful from the perspective of workers, as 'members cherish the temporal-spatial freedom they find in not having to rent their time to a higher authority' (ibid.: 730).

A second area where cooperative organization has continued to play a role in the economy alongside traditional capitalist enterprises is in the financial sector. For instance, in 2011 the International Monetary Fund (2012: 51) estimated that the French mutual sector had assets of €1,606 billion, representing nearly 16 per cent of total assets in the financial sector. In the United Kingdom, the assets of building societies are much lower at just over £325 billion; however, with forty-five societies the sector is nonetheless significant (BSA 2013a), and as of May 2013 British building societies had a 16.4 per cent share of the mortgage market and a 23.9 per cent share of gross lending (BSA 2013b: 1). While it is clear that these institutions remain in a minority in comparison to other forms of banking institution, their endurance over time suggests that they represent a viable alternative form of organization.

In the context of the economic crisis that began in the banking sector in 2008, diversity in the financial sector also appears to offer the prospect of realizing a broad range of benefits because, first, 'Building societies are less prone than banks to pursue risky speculative activity'; secondly, because 'A mixed system is likely to produce a more stable financial sector'; and thirdly, 'A stronger mutual sector will enhance competition within the financial system' (BSA 2009: 4). The claim that mutual financial institutions are more stable reflects the conclusions of an IMF working paper produced in 2007 (Hesse and Cihak 2007: 18), and the notion that institutions that are not readily exposed to the short-term profit motives of shareholders will be more stable seems intuitive. This is because the primary source of capital reserves for cooperative banks is retained earnings, which means that their financial positions are damaged by bad lending and their reserves 'cannot easily be replaced by raising new capital in the market' (BSA 2009: 11).

The idea that a greater number of cooperatives in the financial sector will promote systemic stability may at first appear to need a greater degree of explanation; however, it is equally intuitive. The reason is simply that institutions in the financial system will have different portfolios of risk because different ownership structures will help to avoid the kind of herd behaviour whereby all institutions hold the same or similar types of assets and are affected equally badly in moments of crisis, with repercussions that reverberate through the system. As the UK Building Societies Association (ibid.: 11) put it: 'The more diversified is a financial system in terms of size, ownership and structure of business, the better it is able to weather the strains produced by the normal business cycle, in particular avoiding the bandwagon effect, and the better it is able to adjust to consumer preferences.'

However, like the early cooperative communities, cooperative finance has been prone to degeneration over time, while in the United States their equivalents, the Savings & Loans corporations, were the subject of widespread frauds in the 1980s. Jon Elster (1989a: 94) supposed that some of the reasons workers' cooperatives fail or degenerate are because people do not wish to participate in decision-making or that cooperative firms attract people with insufficient expertise. He also suggests cooperatives may be discriminated against by credit markets (ibid.: 98), and that 'reform experiments might attract unstable individuals, excessive risk-takers, and people lacking in pragmatic orientation' (ibid.: 96). David Miller (1981) has likewise outlined some general reasons why cooperatives fail or degenerate over time. He suggests the early ventures of the Owenite period were in the main unprofitable, and so could survive only until the philanthropists who provided the start-up capital decided to withdraw their support. However, he also notes how cooperative degeneration can stem from financial success. This is because the growing size of capital can see an increasing number of shares passed to outside investors as cooperatives seek to raise money for expansion, which dilutes the cooperative foundations of the society. Finally, he suggests that when small-scale cooperatives succeed and take on new workers, it is tempting to take them on as wage workers rather than partners, so successful cooperatives effectively become mini-capitalist enterprises over time (ibid.: 310–12).

In the cooperative or mutual form, then, it is possible to see an alternative to capitalism that may have potential benefits. Through the expansion of workers' cooperatives it is possible to minimize the extent of alienation as people can take greater job satisfaction from the extra control they have over their working days, and production takes on more of a social purpose. As such, the tendency for capital to erode its own basis through the exploitation and impoverishment of labour would seem to be less, and the crisis dynamics of capitalist social relations muted if not resolved. In the financial sector, money is used for productive investment, especially in housing. The financial practices of mutual firms have generally not included the speculative expansion of credit that fuels overproduction in the capitalist economy, and as such they also appear to have the potential to mute crisis tendencies within capitalism. Even if a fully cooperative economy were not established, a broader range of business structures in finance has the potential to mitigate the undesirable consequences of a crisis because not all financial institutions will be affected in the same way by crises if they have different capital structures. In terms of its relationship to the crisis tendencies in capitalism, then, the cooperative form appears to have a lot to offer.

The degeneration and failure of cooperatives in historical perspective, however, raises the spectre of Nozick's claim that inequality is inevitable in societies where people have different consumption preferences. Practical experience appears to suggest that, over time, people do become more willing to trade the social and civic gains that come from cooperative and mutual association for the kinds of monetary benefit more traditionally associated with capitalist forms of organization. However, rather than indicating a flaw in the cooperative model as such, degeneration is a reflection of the fact that in our everyday actions we constantly make decisions that make and remake the prevailing form of social, economic and political organization. As such, while a cooperative alternative to capitalism might be a desirable form of social, economic and political organization, it is not appropriate to think of it as a desirable *outcome* in itself. Rather, like capitalism, cooperative forms of organization should be seen in terms of their social constitution, as arrangements that are continually remade or resisted through our social actions. If we are to realize and sustain a cooperative alternative to capitalism, it is not enough to make it, we must also continually *remake* it in our everyday actions.

A socialist alternative to capitalism

The notion that competition for profit drives crisis dynamics in capitalism provides a clear rationale for the kind of cooperative economy discussed in the previous section. However, as profit could remain a feature of the cooperative system as alternative forms of production, distribution and exchange operate alongside traditional capitalist enterprises, there is also a case for going farther than this – towards a socialist alternative to capitalism. This section outlines the basis of a socialist form of organization and argues that, just as was the case with the cooperative economy, it should be treated as a process rather than an outcome in itself. This is because even within contemporary socialist movements, there are differing interests that have the potential to re-create injustices within the new form of social organization. This is illustrated briefly through a discussion of the impact of nationalization in historical perspective, and in more detail through a discussion of the gendered nature of production, which has been accepted within working-class movements. This suggests that a transition to a socialist economy would be likely to reproduce such a gendered society. Once again, because capitalism and alternatives to capitalism do not exist outside the people acting in the forms of production, distribution and exchange that they embody, the section argues that we should think about socialism as a form of social relations that needs to be continually made and remade if it is to represent a stable and equitable alternative to capitalism.

Just what exactly a socialist alternative to capitalism would look like is contested. However, it is generally acknowledged that in a socialist economy the means of production would be taken into social ownership, thus ending the exploitation of the wage relation under capitalism, and ending the profit motive that drives the production of commodities for which there is no demand. It would also therefore serve to end the crisis tendency in capitalist social relations as it was understood by Marx. The distribution of goods in this alternative to capitalism would, in its early stages, reflect the relative contributions that each individual has made to the production of goods in society. In other words, each individual would be entitled to the full value of his or her labour. In the more advanced stages of socialism, the distribution would reflect the varying needs of individuals so that each would have access to the goods and services that they need to live well regardless of the contribution that they were able to make to production.

G. A. Cohen (2009: ch. 1) offers a good description of what a socialist economy would look like by offering a camping trip as a metaphor. He notes how, on a camping trip, there is no leader of the group and everybody is equal in hierarchical terms. The group is motivated by the shared desire that each person on the camping trip has a good time doing things that they like to do, whether that be as an individual, or as part of the group. On a camping trip, Cohen notes, people take all of the things that they need to have a good time, including things to cook with, and items to amuse themselves. 'As is usual on camping trips' (ibid.: 3–4), he notes, 'we avail ourselves of those facilities collectively: even if they are privately owned things, they are under collective control for the duration of the trip.' Each person understands the conditions under which it is acceptable to use these items and for what purposes, and they are used for a collective endeavour. 'Somebody fishes, somebody else prepares the food, and another person cooks it. People who hate cooking but enjoy washing up may do all the washing up, and so on' (ibid.: 4). Even if you were not an egalitarian, Cohen suggests, the principles of equality and reciprocity would be accepted because 'to question them would contradict the spirit of the trip' (ibid.: 5).

In the moves towards a socialist economy, it is therefore important to ask whether moves towards socializing ownership of the means of production also serve to socialize the benefits of production. An interesting example of this conjuncture can be seen in the debate about the benefits of the nationalization of industry in Britain in the periods after the Second World War. In the years 1945–51, large sections of British infrastructure and heavy industry, including telecommunications, coal, iron and steel, electricity, gas and transportation, were taken into public ownership. At one level, these measures could be interpreted as significant moves towards the socialization of the economy, especially when taken in conjunction with the significant reforms to social security that were introduced in the form of the welfare state. By 1951 approximately two million people in Britain were employed by the public sector and approximately 20 per cent of the British economy was under public control (Coates 1975: 44). The government also attempted to take control of sectors that remained in private hands through a system of planning, whereby a Capital Issues Committee would direct investment to areas that it deemed of particular importance. For instance, works to factories costing over £1,000 would need to be licensed, and the consumption of raw materials would be directed towards key sectors (ibid.: 45). On the surface, it appears that moves towards a socialized economy were put firmly in process.

However, it is also possible to develop an alternative view. Simon Clarke (2011 [1988]: loc. 3938) noted how both the working class and government committees had made strong calls for nationalization in Britain before the 1940s and 1950s, at the end of the First World War. Nonetheless, 'There was nothing inherently socialist', he argued, 'in the proposal for nationalisation.' This is because the rationale for nationalization lay not in the desirability of the move towards a socialized economy, but in its ability to rationalize capitalist enterprises. As he puts it:

> Public ownership had long been established as the form through which the state limited the ability of particular capitals to exploit

monopoly powers. It was a remedy that had already been well tested as a means of restructuring capital and rationalising supply in the bus and tram, gas, water and electricity industries, where the duplication of facilities had led to chronic excess capacity. (Ibid.: loc. 3952)

In light of the historical experience of nationalization, the nature of the industries that the British state took control of after the Second World War is therefore revealing. By the time of the post-war nationalizations British heavy industry had been in decline for over fifty years and was struggling with its international competitiveness. These industries had also suffered from further degeneration during the war, and were in need of levels of investment that private capitalists were either unwilling or unable to provide. The form of the nationalizations was also interesting, because while the government established liability for the required investment in these industries, previous owners were, in the main, retained in salaried managerial positions. In light of the subsequent privatizations of these same industries, it is therefore possible to paint a different picture of the consequences of nationalization; rather than it contributing to the socialization of the economy, it appears that the government socialized the costs of post-war reconstruction and British relative economic decline, before returning industries to private hands, which in turn allowed those who were already at the top end of the income pyramid to reap the financial benefits of government's investment in declining industries while sharing the cost.

The extent to which temporary nationalizations have arguably been used in order to subsidize investments that serve to benefit privileged members of society as much and if not more than they do working people and their families illustrates an interesting point. It suggests that the *means* that a government introduces cannot be judged in terms of its merits independently of the *ends* that it is trying to achieve. This is because while the means of nationalization might appear to be a step towards socialized ownership, it has in fact been used to achieve things that stand in stark relief to this aim. This illustrates the extent to which it is important to think of alternatives to capitalism as processes that are made and remade by the actions of people, including legislators where they are involved, that must continue to be remade to avoid undesirable or suboptimal consequences of reform.

It is not simply in the degeneration of small moves towards socialization of the economy that this problem lies. Differentiated interests within classes also mean that transition towards alternative forms of social, economic and political organization has the potential to re-create inequalities and the undesirable social consequences associated with them if they are not addressed. For instance, even within the working-class movement there has been a strong tendency for the role of women to be subordinated to the role of men in relation to the means of production, which has been endorsed and sustained through the structures of working-class representation, participation and activism.

The origins of the notion that women's relationship to the economy and society more broadly is different from men's began with the utopian socialists, and especially Henry de Saint-Simon and his followers. They argued that 'Society had left the moral-loving-artistic faculty underdeveloped, keeping women, who excelled in this faculty, in severe subjugation' (Goldstein 1982: 96). John Cunliffe and Andrew Reeve (1996: 63) noted how 'For some members of the school, the exploitation of women by men was more acute even that that experienced by direct economic producers', and they therefore proposed abolishing gendered rights to inheritance and gender equality in public life (ibid.: 74). However, this group of socialists also believed that the benefits could only be realized if 'women stay as sweet as they are' and, as such, 'the Saint-Simonians opposed emancipating "la femme" until the world became feminized' (Goldstein 1982: 96). Ultimately, 'The feminism of the Saint-Simonians, then, was a sharply-double edged sword. Women needed autonomy, but the purpose of this autonomy was to ensure that society establish roles suited to the gentle, sweet, and ultimately weak, nature of women' (ibid.: 97).

As such, Goldstein (ibid.: 97) has quipped, 'With friends like the Saint-Simonians did women's liberation need enemies?' This exposition of early socialist feminism is particularly astute with regard to a key point. Namely, while socialists of the eighteenth century recognized the exploitation of capitalist social relations, their imaginations of future society saw the liberation of women only within the limits of perceptions of their essential physical characteristics.

Later, Frederick Engels (2004 [1884]: 79) suggested that the formal inequality of men and women before the law was the 'effect of the economic oppression of women' that began in the 'patriarchal family, and even more with the monogamian individual family'. He argued that, under capitalism, household administration had become 'a *private service*' with married women becoming 'the first domestic servant, pushed out of participation in social production' (ibid.: 80). Women were faced with a contradiction, he suggested, between their roles in social production and the ability to earn a living and their 'family duties', which meant 'the man has to be the earner [that] gives him a dominating position which requires no special legal privileges'. Through this contradiction, he argued, the bourgeois role within the family was conferred on men (ibid.: 80). As such, Engels (ibid.: 80) believed that 'the first premise for the emancipation of women is the reintroduction of the entire female into public industry'.

Like utopian socialist feminism, however, Marxist feminism stemming from the work of Engels is not without its problems. Veronica Beechey (1977: 57), for instance, noted how Engels does not consider the gendered division of labour within the family to be problematic, or the role of the state in excluding women from paid employment in social production, but simply assumes that patriarchy will end with women's participation in the labour force. More broadly, then, Marxist feminism has been criticized for its tendency to 'subsume the feminist struggle to the "larger" struggle against capital' (Hartmann 1979: 1). Heidi Hartmann (ibid.: 4) argued that while 'aware of the deplorable situation of women in their time the early Marxists failed to focus on the *differences* between men's and women's experiences under capitalism. They did not focus on feminist questions – how and why women are oppressed as women.' It is clear that, in contrast to Engels' predictions, even as women have increasingly been incorporated into the paid labour force, this has not occurred in a way providing equal status for men and women (ibid.: 4; CSE Sex and Class Group 1982: 85). There are at least three areas where it is clear that women have historically occupied a place subordinate to men within the working class. These relate, respectively, to women's position relative to men in the industrial reserve army of unemployed; women's position relative to men with respect to skilled and unskilled labour; and women's position relative to men with respect to unpaid domestic labour.

On the first of these issues, Jane Humphries (1983: 8, emphasis in original) has noted that 'female employment is more *cyclically* volatile than total unemployment', which means that in times when unemployment is increasing, the unemployment of women increases proportionately more than the unemployment of men. As such, women have been described as a latent labour reserve who 'like precapitalist industrial workers initially constituted a pool of unexploited labour hidden in the sense of not representing a drain on the capitalist surplus, but able to respond to the demands of the economy' (ibid.: 14). There are a number of historical examples where this has manifested itself. The First World War, for instance, 'was a period in which large numbers of women, both single and married, entered into paid employment in the centres of modern industry, since female labour as part of the industrial reserve army of labour was pressed into service during the wartime labour short-age' (Beechey 1977: 55). However, at the end of the war, when men who had gone into military service returned, the women who had entered into paid employment met resistance to their roles from the trade union movement. For instance, in the United Kingdom, the engineering union brokered agreements with the government and employers stipulating that women should leave jobs at the end of the war 'since these were men's jobs' (ibid.: 55). Within the working class there was therefore a clear gender divide that resulted in the separate unionization of men and women even within industries. In the sense that women are perceived as 'marginal workers', they are also seen as 'marginal trade unionists' (CSE Sex and Class Group 1982: 87), and therefore subordinate to men in the movement that is most active in attempts to realize a socialist alternative to capitalism.

Even as the paid employment of women has become more wide-spread outside times of war, it is possible to observe gendered patterns within the division of labour. For instance, 'Where there is a skilled/unskilled divide, the presence of women may be noted on the unskilled side' (ibid.: 85). Again, this was manifested in the British engineering industry during the First World War in the form of agreements barring women from entry to skilled professions in anything other than the most exceptional circumstances (Beechey 1977: 55). More generally, it has been noted that

> Machinery is designed, built, maintained, and even operated, overwhelmingly, by men. Even when women operate machinery it is in a sense only 'lent' to them by men, who remain the mechanics and maintenance engineers. Male grasp of technology dequalified women just as capital's technicians and scientists dequalify workers. (CSE Sex and Class Group 1982: 86)

Despite views of the firm as 'a gender-neutral actor that can undermine local gender inequalities by incorporating women into the (again, gender-neutral) market economy' (Elias 2006: 92–3), it has been possible for feminist researchers to identify clear examples of gendered recruitment within the workplace. For instance, in a study of recruitment practices at a multinational firm that manufactures clothing in Malaysia, Juanita Elias (ibid.: 98) found that management 'frequently made the claim that women show greater neatness, care and patience in their work in comparison to their male counterparts', and used recruitment processes that aimed to identify skills such as 'neatness and care, patience and an ability to put up with repetitive work, a good eye, dexterity, speed and an ability to follow simple instructions'. These are skills and qualities, Elias (ibid.: 98) noted, that 'are regarded either as innate to women or skills developed in the household from an early age'. The notion that the firm or the marketplace is gender neutral, therefore, is undermined by practice, which still clearly reinforces the view that some work is 'women's work'. For instance, within the firm Elias (ibid.: 99) studied, 98.1 per cent of sewing machinists were female.

Finally, it has frequently been noted that women traditionally perform a far greater proportion of domestic labour than men. A 1990 survey of the domestic divisions of labour in Greater Manchester was particularly revealing in this area. For instance, it showed that women overwhelmingly carried out routine housework tasks such as tidying up, vacuuming, cooking and cleaning lavatories (Warde and

Hetherington 1993: 31). The same was true of childcare tasks such as bathing children and changing nappies (ibid.: 31). Overall, the study found a 'very strong sense of what are men's, and what are women's tasks', and even when there were exceptions to the general rule, these exceptions 'seemed to be essentially haphazard and probably the result of circumstantial pressures' (ibid.: 43). While a more recent study revealed that between 1975 and 1997 there was a reduction in the proportion of domestic labour performed by women from 77 per cent to 63 per cent (Sullivan 2000: 443), the gap is still substantial. This same study showed that in terms of time commitments, women spent around 210 minutes per day cooking and cleaning in 1975 in comparison to just 18 minutes per day spent on these tasks by men. By 1997 this figure had fallen to 132 minutes per day for women and increased to 31 minutes per day for men, indicating a continuation of the gendered division of domestic labour (ibid.: 445, Table 3) in a context where the absolute gains experienced by women could very well be explained by domestic labour-saving machinery rather than shifts in social attitudes (see Chang 2010: 31–40).

In order to see the significance of this for the socialist alternative to capitalism, it is necessary to ask who benefits from this situation. On the one hand, capitalists clearly benefit from the subordinate position occupied by women in relation to the means of production. Female wage labour serves to lower the cost of labour-power overall because these costs can be spread across the whole working population rather than just the male working population. This effect is amplified because of the tradition of male 'breadwinning', which means that married women's wages can be kept especially low because they can look to their husbands to meet needs that are not met by their wage income (Beechey 1977: 51). However, as Heidi Hartmann (1979: 6) noted in her answer to the question of who benefits from the subordination of the role of women to men under capitalists, the answer is 'Surely capitalists, but also surely men, who as husbands and fathers received personalized services at home.'

Men's control over access to employment and education opportunities, which serves to reinforce the way in which children are socialized into gender roles and are social phenomena, is particularly important. This is because changes in the way in which commodities are produced – for instance through public ownership of the means of production – does not appear to have a necessary connection to the way in which people are socialized. As such, 'society could undergo transition from capitalism to socialism, for example, and remain patriarchal' (ibid.: 13). Indeed, this scenario appears likely if we consider the possibility that working men recognize that working women are competition for their own jobs, as well as 'their very wives, who could not "serve two masters" very well' (ibid.: 15). Valerie Bryson (2004: 17) has therefore noted that Marxist feminism 'could not see that the interests and priorities of working-class women and men might at times conflict [...] that working-class men might benefit from women's subordination, and that they might therefore have an interest in maintaining it, even in a socialist society'. As Bryson (ibid.: 21) phrases it, 'men have a lot to lose if they are displaced as the central starting point of culture, knowledge and economic planning, and if they are required to forgo their greater access to leisure time and relative freedom from domestic chores and caring responsibilities'. 'Men', Hartmann (1979: 24) wrote, 'have more to lose than their chains.'

It seems clear that the gendered division of labour exists even within structures of working-class representation, participation and activism. As such, to assume that the acceptance of such inequalities would disintegrate in a transition towards socialism seems questionable. It is not clear that any socialism that has been struggled for or is being struggled for is the same for men as it is for women, who continue to occupy subordinate roles within the working class specifically and in relation to the means of production more broadly. If G. A. Cohen's kind of camping-trip socialism were to be achieved, therefore, it is unlikely to represent the kind of harmonious outcomes that he imagined in principle because the transition itself is likely to re-create inequalities that exist in the prevailing form of capitalism, especially when they are treated (as gender equality often has been by socialists) as subordinate to the issue of class.

This suggests that socialism, as an alternative to capitalism, is unlikely to represent a desirable alternative to capitalism for all people. This is because the prevailing form of production, distribution and exchange is constituted by the social activities of individuals within it. As such, as long as some people have pejorative interests and assumptions that go unchallenged, it is likely that any alternative form of production, distribution and exchange will re-create at least some of them. Even if it were possible for socialism to be made by people in response to the perceived inefficiencies and injustices of capitalism, it would be necessary for people to continue to challenge those aspects of social relations that continue to produce inequality and injustice. In this sense, like the other alternatives to capitalism that this chapter has discussed, socialism should be perceived as a process that must be continually made and remade in the image of the interests of the people that constitute it, rather than as an end-point or outcome to follow capitalism.

Conclusions

This chapter has presented three alternatives to the prevailing form of capitalism. The first, libertarianism, constitutes an alternative capitalism in the sense that it attempts to enhance the operation of actually existing forms of production, distribution and exchange. The second and third, cooperative and socialist organization, constitute alternatives *to* capitalism because they challenge the operation of the prevailing form of production, distribution and exchange. Two important points follow from the discussion of the alternatives presented here. The first of these relates to the *form* that any alternative (to) capitalism should take, and the second to how we should perceive varying forms of social organization.

As this book has argued that capitalism itself is a fundamentally crisis-prone form of social organization, it rejects the possibility of realizing a socially sustainable libertarian alternative capitalism. Even if claims that libertarian theorists have made about the basis of private property and justice in transfer can be justified in theory, it has argued that inequality stemming from such arrangements would ultimately prove unbearable. The book's argument therefore advocates the creation of social relationships that are driven by the production of socially useful goods rather than the accumulation of profit, and both the cooperative and socialist alternatives to capital-ism discussed in this chapter are founded on similar logics. However, this does not mean that a 'cooperative' or 'socialist' alternative to capitalism will represent in any traditional sense a utopia. Both suffer from various problems, related to issues of sustainability and the reproduction of injustices that exist within capitalism, in the new form of social organization. To argue that an alternative to capitalism could represent a utopia, a thing, to be achieved, is to neglect the social constitution of economy and society; it is to stop recognizing that the realization of desirable outcomes is the product of our interactions with one another on a daily basis. No matter what alternatives to capitalism exist or are realized, it is necessary to continue reflecting on the nature and consequences of the social relations that exist so that we can continue to make active decisions about whether we decide to remake or resist the world we live in. This is as true of any alternative to capitalism as it is of capitalism itself.

4 | ANTI-CAPITALISM

Introduction

The previous chapter considered one alternative capitalism and two alternatives to capitalism. It argued that while libertarianism offered a theoretically consistent alternative capitalism that *might* be justified on the basis of neoliberal political economy, it was likely to generate vast inequalities that would contribute to generating instability in capitalist social relations. It then considered cooperative and socialist alternatives to capitalism, and suggested that the degeneration of early cooperative communities and the extent to which a gendered division of labour has often been accepted *within* the socialist movement mean it is necessary to think of alternatives to capitalism as *processes* that must be continually made and remade if they are not to degenerate into crisis-prone capitalistic forms of social organization, or if they are not to reproduce undesirable features of capitalist social relations. This chapter considers the ways in which capitalism can be resisted, and an alternative to capitalism made and remade; in other words, the practice of anti-capitalism.

The first section of the chapter develops a theory of the state, and argues that the state should be thought of in terms of the social relationships that constitute it. In light of the fact that the prevailing form of these social relationships is capitalist, it suggests that the state should be viewed as a capitalist state. In light of this analysis, the chapter then considers the prospects for an alternative to capitalism to be achieved *within*, *through* and *against* the state. Through a discussion of the ideas of people such as Robert Owen, Ralph Miliband, Rosa Luxemburg and Vladimir Lenin, it considers the potential of reformist and revolutionary modes of anti-capitalism of different forms, but argues through a reflection on the work of John Holloway that the most important feature of anti-capitalist action is the recognition that the world is socially constituted, and that maintaining democratic and pluralistic approaches to anti-capitalism is of fundamental importance if oppressive forms of social organization are not to be re-created. In contrast to the 'top-down' paternalistic and revolutionary approaches of anti-capitalist action within and through the state, it argues for anti-capitalist action to occur from the 'bottom up' through experimentation. It suggests that an awareness of the socially constituted nature of the state and economy provides an impetus to do things differently, and encourages a continued reflection on the consequences of social action, which can help to guard against degeneration into capitalism or the reproduction of oppressive social relationships that have affected paternalistic and revolutionary forms of anti-capitalism.

The capitalist state

Like capitalism itself, the state is something that it is easy to take for granted. However, the way in which we conceive of the state is important for the way in which we assess its potential to facilitate change. One way to do this is to consider the democratic state as an arbiter between differing interests in society. In this conception, elected politicians and permanent officials in the civil service work together in order to come to an assessment of the balance of preferences in society and act, insofar as is possible, to bring them to pass. This does not mean that the state becomes a mere reflection of the aggregate interest; rather actors in power within the state continue to make judgements reflecting the feasibility of certain objectives, and attempt to prevent outcomes where the pursuit of interests that are individually rational do produce collectively irrational outcomes. This reflects Edmund Burke's (1774) famous observation that a representative of the people should exercise their judgement and 'betrays, instead of serving you, if he sacrifices it to your opinion'.

In such a conception, the state can be seen as a 'black box' that performs the function of mediating between inputs in a particular way, and produces policy outputs on this basis. In terms of explaining domestic policy-making, then, policy outputs can be seen as a reflection of the weight afforded to the views of varying interest groups. In terms of recent debates about globalization, this kind of understanding has been reflected in the idea that the power of global capital has increased to such an extent that the discretion states have to make policy is significantly constrained. This is manifested in the notion that states have been forced to become 'competition states' (Cerny 1991, 1997) and that there is an intrinsic conflict between exchange rate stability, currency convertibility and monetary policy autonomy (Andrews 1994; Cohen 1998; Chapter 2 above). From a critical perspective, it is reflected clearly in Stephen Gill and David Law's (1989) claim that global finance has been able to achieve a hegemonic status, and states must respond to the structural power of capital because of the greater costs they face from an investment strike than from a labour strike. From both perspectives, it is through the relative ascendancy of market power vis-à-vis the state that the tendency for governments to introduce market-facilitating policies has been explained.

In the 1960s, Ralph Miliband attempted to explain this phenomenon – the tendency for the state to act in the broad interests of capital – by 'confronting liberal political theorists of democracy with the "facts" about the social background, personal ties and shared values of economic and political elites' (Jessop 1990: 29–30). In doing so, he was able to demonstrate that people in positions of power overwhelmingly share a similar privileged background, and on this basis argued that the state can be characterized as an instrument of a ruling capitalist class, which allowed it to act in the interest of capitalism in general. However, the need for the state to possess the ability 'to take actions against the particular interests of capitalists' if it is to act in the interests of capitalism in general (Block 1987: 53) – accounting for its 'relative autonomy' – is something that critics suggested that Miliband's analysis cannot explain.

Most famously, Nicos Poulantzas (1969: 74) argued that observations of connections between the social backgrounds of political elites with those of the dominant capitalist class cannot account for the ability of the state to act in this way. It was Poulantzas' view that if members of the ruling class dominate the state it is because the economic structure allows them to. As he phrased it, 'the direct participation of members of the ruling class in the State apparatus is not the *cause* but the *effect*, and moreover, a chance and contingent one' (ibid.: 73, emphasis in original). In other words, Poulantzas argued that the state was a *capitalist* state because the economic structure made it a capitalist state. In response, Miliband (1970: 57) argued that the emphasis on the role of the economic structure in Poulantzas' work was unhelpful because the idea that the objective structures of the economy led to groups of people from certain classes occupying key positions within the state implies that 'the state is not "manipulated" by the ruling class into doing its bidding: it does so autonomously but totally because of the "objective relations" imposed upon it by the system' (ibid.: 57). This, he argued, can be described as a kind of structural super-determinism in which the economy absolutely determines politics, and as a result undermines agency in political and economic processes.

According to Fred Block (1987: 53), Poulantzas' conception of the relative autonomy of the state that is developed in terms of the structures of the economy is equally problematic because the nature and limits of the state's autonomy cannot be defined. As he phrases it:

> Relative autonomy theories assume that the ruling class will respond effectively to the state's abuse of that autonomy. But for the ruling class to be capable of taking such corrective actions, it must have some degree of political cohesion, an understanding of its general interests, and a high degree of political sophistication [...] yet if the ruling class or a segment of it is class-conscious, then the degree of the autonomy of the state is clearly quite limited. (Ibid.: 53)

In other words, relative autonomy theories of the capitalist state collapse back into themselves when attempts are made to define the limits of that autonomy. In this respect, Bob Jessop (1990: 103) argued that 'the concept of "relative autonomy" as a principle of explanation can be consigned to the theoretical dustbin'.

Each of these conceptualizations of the state, to a greater or lesser extent, treats it as a sphere of activity that stands outside the market, and implies that power can shift between the two. However, treating the state and market as two separate spheres of activity neglects the social basis of their existence – the fact that neither the state nor the market exists outside of the human social interactions that constitute them. As such, it is necessary to conceive of both state and market in terms of the social processes that continually make and remake them. As Matthew Watson (2005: 21) has noted, the emphasis on the autonomy of states and markets 'at the point of constitution [...] does nothing to address the possibility that political and economic activities are co-constituted within a single social reality'. In order to do so, he argues, it is necessary to approach the problem of the state through the lens of the co-constitutive nature of political and economic action, rather than through a debate that has been 'couched in terms of the causal relationship between one entity called "states" and another called "markets"' (ibid.: 21).

In other words, to understand the state it is necessary to understand the nature of the social relationships that constitute it – capitalist social relations. As Peter Burnham (1995: 93) has noted, the state 'is not autonomous, or simply *related* to "the economy", rather it is an integral aspect of the set of social relations whose overall form is determined by the manner in which the extraction of surplus from the immediate producer is secured'. John Holloway (2005: 13) likewise notes: 'The fact that work is organised on a capitalist basis means that what the state does and can do is limited and shaped by the need to maintain the capitalist system of which it is a part.'

As established in Chapter 1, the capitalist social relations that constitute the state and give rise to its existence as the political form of accumulation are dependent on the double freedom of workers so that capitalists are able to extract surplus value from them to create profit. We then saw in Chapter 2 how these social relationships are contradictory in the context of competition and the tendency to engage in accumulation for accumulation's sake, as capital progressively undermines the basis of its existence – labour. On this basis, it can be argued that 'The state is not a state *in a capitalist society*, but rather a moment of the class antagonism of capital and labour' (Bonefeld 1992: 113, my emphasis). In other words, the state does not sit within capitalism. Rather, it is the political form of the class antagonisms that characterize capitalist social relations.

On this basis, the state can be described in terms of its role in 'defining and enforcing collectively binding decisions upon the members of a territorially defined society in the name of their common interest' (Burnham 1994: 3). Under capitalist social relations, this means that the state 'mediates capital's dependence on the reproduction of labour power within the limits of capital' (Bonefeld 1992: 119). As such, the laissez-faire, Keynesian and neoliberal periods can be understood as *forms* of state where governments employed differing strategies in order to attempt to mediate the contradictions and antagonisms of capitalist social relations. The deflationary consequences of the gold standard, the concessions to full employment under embedded liberalism, and financialization in the wake of neoliberal austerity can therefore all be seen as modes of legitimizing the exploitation of labour without fundamentally addressing the class antagonism between capital and labour and the crisis tendencies therein. However, although the state is a form of the prevailing social relations, there is no reason to assume that its characteristics are 'immutable or functionally determined' (Burnham 1994: 1) because the relations that constitute the state are in a constant state of crisis. As such, if we perceive Marxism and its theory of the state 'not just as a theory of oppression but also, and above all, a theory of social instability', then Marxism itself should be perceived as 'an open theory' (Holloway 1992: 147). On this basis, the theory also presents the possibility of substantive change in capitalist social relations to an alternative to capitalism. In light of this analysis of the state, the next three sections of this chapter examine the potential for this change to be achieved *within*, *through* and *against* the state.

Within the state

The practice of anti-capitalism can be undertaken *within* the state in a number of different ways, but each of these shares in common the view that it is necessary neither for anti-capitalists to seize state power nor to dismantle its structures. Rather, an alternative to capitalism can be realized through a variety of means within the prevailing legal and political framework, through the action of philanthropists, trade unions and political parties, facilitated by state policy.

Philanthropy, paternalism and cooperative communities One way that a transition to an alternative to capitalism might be achieved is through a combination of the philanthropy of industrialists who recognize the benefits to be gained from having a well-treated labour force, and government action to assist in the creation of a social environment in which people are helped to realize the benefits of living their lives in a way that allows them to maximize their contribution to the civic, social and pecuniary aims of the community. This was the approach favoured by Robert Owen in the creation of his cooperative communities. As Chapter 3 established, Owen believed that social reform could begin with the philanthropy of industrialists who would place a greater emphasis on the well-being of their workers, who would in turn develop 'good character' through the structures this philanthropy provided. Ultimately, benefits would be realized for all of society through this structure as people more clearly recognized what was in their own interests.

The basis of Owen's desire to address what he perceived to be the major social problems of his time was his view that the majority of the people in the United Kingdom – the workers – were 'permitted to be very generally formed without proper guidance and direction' (Owen 1991: 10). In other words, he believed that the lack of a proper education meant that people were not able to recognize their own interests and the interests of their community and it was from this that social problems stemmed. In associating problems such as crime and poverty with the way in which people were socialized and educated, rather than ascribing them to the innate characteristics of certain individuals or groups of individuals, Owen's conception of society also produced a clear programme for the development and betterment of society, which began with education. The principal means through which social reform could take place in Owen's eyes, therefore, would be through the establishment of 'rational plans for the education and general formation of the characters of their subjects. *These plans must be devised to train children from their earliest infancy in good habits of every description* [...] *They must afterwards be rationally educated, and their labour usefully directed*' (ibid.: 16, emphasis in original).

More specifically, this translated into a call for governments to provide training and employment through a 'national system for the formation of character' and programmes of public works to provide a 'reserve of employment for the surplus working classes' (ibid.: 35). It was suggested that the formation of good character could be most efficiently achieved through the removal of children 'so far as is at present practicably, from the erroneous treatment of the yet untrained and untaught parents', to be cared for by others during the daytime before returning home at night. Children would benefit from learning the 'best habits and principles' in play areas provided for the purposes of amusement and recreation, which would also be beneficial to parents because it would give them more free time (ibid.: 39–40). In such a proposal, it is possible to see the origins of a national system of education that would be charged with preparing people for the exigencies of life in the contemporary world, facilitated by philanthropic industrialists and catalysed by government action.

Social reform, however, would not be limited to the philanthropic work of capitalists helping the masses to realize their own interests, facilitated by government programmes of education. Structures for the punishment and prevention of crime would also be important given Owen's view that character is shaped by circumstances and not innately given. Because he believed that if society was to be harmonious people needed to learn standards of good behaviour that they had until then had little opportunity to develop, Owen argued that the government should set limits to 'the consumption of ardent spirits', which he suggested were a means 'to seduce the ignorant and wretched' (ibid.: 65), as well as undertaking the prohibition of gambling, reform of provision for the poor, and penal reform (ibid.: 65). On the basis of his view that the principal problems with society stemmed from a general ignorance of the majority about what was best for them, and his view that these moral standards could be taught, Owen believed that there was a clear role for the government to play in assisting in the development of society by this means: 'The end of government', after all, Owen (ibid.: 62) stated, 'is to make the governed and the governors happy.'

The emphasis in Owen's programme to create a new form of society therefore lies in the ability of both capitalists and workers to be socialized so that they might realize the benefits to be had for all people that would come from supplementing the profit motive with an equal concern for social and civic goals. If philanthropists could be convinced to provide the start-up capital, and government assisted them with their intentions to develop the human character by establishing educational institutions, and other social reforms, it would be possible to move towards a cooperative alternative to capitalism.

However, other left-wing reformists found this programme of anti-capitalism within the state to be problematic. As J. K. Gibson-Graham (2003: 133) has noted, it was felt by other socialists that 'in the face of the "realities" of capitalist power Owen's belief in the transformative effects of pedagogy seemed weak and myopic'. A host of concerns were also raised about Owen's vision for reform. For instance, questions were asked about how a cooperative economy (as opposed to a cooperative industry) could operate without individual sectors emphasizing their own importance over other sectors, and reflecting this by providing levels of pay or conditions of work above the average which fostered undesirable competition between sectors. It was also thought that cooperatives would use this 'group individualism' to continue to extract profit, and that the psychology of leadership would make it impossible for disputes to be resolved on the basis of worker control (Webb and Webb summarized in ibid.: 137). Each of these criticisms relates to the problems of cooperative degeneration that were raised in Chapter 3, and suggests that the sustainability of the cooperative economy achieved principally through philanthropy and education is extremely questionable.

However, beyond these practical objections, Owen's programme for reform within the prevailing structures of the state can be criticized on the grounds that it relies on a paternalism that has the clear potential to re-create certain aspects of capitalist oppression. This is because it would be the capitalist philanthropists and the government facilitating the institutional structures of education who set the standards of moral behaviour that would benefit society. Decisions about certain kinds of social activity, such as drinking alcohol and gambling, but more fundamentally the education and care of children, would be decided *on behalf* of the majority of people and not by them. Such rigid structures represent a moral position that associates the plight of the poor with their ignorance of what is good for them, couched entirely in terms of the views held by social, economic and political elites. In light of the conception of the state as a *capitalist state*, this is problematic because the design of the institutions for reform is likely to reproduce certain oppressive structures of capitalism. The practice of anti-capitalism within the state on the basis of Owen's vision of cooperative communities and 'a new moral world' – and particularly its paternalistic and 'top-down' approach – could therefore be perceived as a different way of subjugating the views of workers to the views and interests of the wealthy in society.

Parliamentary socialism Other critics of capitalism have argued for the importance of seeking reform through the process of democratic elections. This strand of thought was represented by the Fabian tradition in the United Kingdom, and by social democrats like Karl Kautsky and Eduard Bernstein in continental Europe. Bernstein (1899), for instance, argued that Marx and Engels' predictions about the evolution of capitalism in *The Communist Manifesto* had proved to be incorrect. In particular, he argued that the numbers of the propertied classes were increasing and capitalism was not seeing 'a decreasing number of large capitalists but an increasing number of capitalists of all degrees'. Alongside this growth of the bourgeoisie, Bernstein noted that concessions in terms of factory legislation and trade union legislation meant that 'the needs and opportunities of great political catastrophes are diminished'. In other words, the seizure of state power by workers in order to realize an end to their exploitation would not be necessary. Revolutionary action, he argued, would serve only to hinder the gains being made through the democratic process. '[D]emocracy is,' Bernstein (ibid.) argued, 'at any given time, as much government by the working classes as these are capable of practising according to their intellectual ripeness and the degree of social development that they have attained.'

In the context of the Russian revolution, Karl Kautsky (1918: ch. II) also favoured the pursuit of socialism through democratic means. In his view, it was a mistake to view socialism and democracy as an end and as a means respectively; rather he viewed them both as 'means to the same end' – 'the abolition of every kind of exploitation and oppression, be it directed against a class, a party, a sex, or a race'. He noted that should the democratic popularity of the proletariat increase to such an extent, the ruling class would respond through attempts to suppress democracy and that on this basis it was a 'necessity for the proletariat to defend democracy tooth and nail'. Should they do so and public opinion shift decisively in favour of the proletariat, it would become increasingly difficult for the capitalist class to suppress the workers' movement through the democratic state form. It did not matter that the state was a capitalist state, because changes in representation achieved through democratic means could shift this balance.

Reformists in continental Europe therefore put forward a straight-forward argument for anti-capitalist action within the state that drew on a critique of Marxist understandings of the evolution of social relations under capitalism. These traditions were supplemented in the British Fabian movement by a belief in the necessity of expertise for the purposes of successful government. This position was well captured by Harold J. Laski in the early 1930s. He noted that philosophers such as Thomas Jefferson and Jeremy Bentham had 'too easily assume[d] not only an inherent rightness in their opinions of the multitude but also an instinctive wisdom in its choices', to the extent that 'From their philosophy was born the dangerous inference that any man, without training in affairs, could hope usefully to control their operation' (Laski 1931: 3). It was therefore his view that coming to correct policy decisions depended upon 'accepting the advice of the disinterested expert', and that 'The more elbow-room the latter possesses, the more likely we are to arrive at adequate decisions' (ibid.: 3). As such, Fabianism afforded privilege to those who had reached a certain level of education and in the process represented a form of political conservatism, as these people were likely to stem from the more affluent in society. However, it was also argued that 'it is one thing to urge the need for expert consultation at every stage of making policy; it is another thing, and a very different thing, to insist that the expert's judgement must be final' (ibid.: 4). Fabianism therefore imagined putting those with expertise to work for the benefit of the labour movement as it strove to alleviate the problems of capitalism. In political terms, this manifested itself in a firm belief in the principles of parliamentary socialism, where action through the elected representatives of the state on the basis of their expertise was preferred to direct action by the workers, since these experts were more likely to have a fuller grasp of the situation than those who had not had the benefit of their training.

In practice, this created a situation where the upper ranks of

the British Labour Party became populated by professional politicians and individuals 'who, for one reason or another (and the
reasons were endlessly various) no longer found either the Liberal
or Conservative Party suitable vehicles for their private and public
aspirations' (Miliband 1972: 94). After the First World War, then, it
quickly became clear that 'a majority of Labour leaders remained as
timid and cautious after the war as they had been before, in some
ways more', and that 'the organized working class was far ahead
of its leadership in its willingness to challenge the Government'
(ibid.: 74). Despite having the leadership of the British government
under Ramsay MacDonald twice in the interwar period, the Labour
Party had only a modest record in government in terms of achieving
meaningful moves towards socialism. Miliband (ibid.: 96) explains
some of this caution by the ability of Westminster and its trappings
to seduce those who found themselves in power:

> However, important though were the climate of the House of
> Commons and the 'aristocratic embrace' in taming so many
> Labour members, such influences would not have been nearly so
> effective had these members brought with them to Westminster,
> not only social indignation, but a clearly defined socialist ideol-
> ogy. This they conspicuously lacked.

In other words, members of the British Labour Party with privileged
positions within the institutions of the state appeared to have been
co-opted by the capitalist establishment by the time they achieved
power.

Similar criticisms have been made of twenty-first-century Latin
American socialism, including the governments of Evo Morales in
Bolivia and Rafael Correa in Ecuador. As Amy Kennemore and Gregory
Weeks (2011: 2) noted, although both governments were democratic-
ally elected, after which 'the new leaders enacted bold reforms that
reversed the neoliberal policies of the past, redistributed the nation's
wealth into the hands of marginalised classes, and established new
constitutions through direct democratic practices', such twenty-first-
century socialism 'does not completely reject capitalism'. Rather, it
'rejects market policies imposed by any foreign source'. They note
how the Bolivian Movemiento al Socialismo has been subject to

criticism for its isolation of indigenous movements, and because nationalizations and the new constitution have not challenged the basis of neoliberalism (ibid.: 4–5). Rather, nationalizations in oil and gas have formed 'contracts of shared production' that allow 'oil companies to carry out exploration and exploitation activities independently in the name of the state company' (ibid.: 5), while revenues from oil and gas remain highly dependent on the volatility of global commodity prices and the propensity for foreign firms to invest in Bolivia in the context of the nationalization programme (ibid.: 5). In Ecuador, Correa similarly increased social expenditure, initially financed through taxes on foreign firms. However, this forced the budget into deficit by 2008, and encouraged Ecuador to search for new external finance and encourage renewed foreign investment (ibid.: 9) on essentially capitalistic terms.

Meanwhile, Hugo Chávez's government in Venezuela has also been criticized for the extent to which it failed to challenge the basis of capitalist state power, as tension between the radical activists and the state has manifested itself as 'Chávez supporters in communities [...] end up in bitter conflicts with state functionaries who try to implement the top-down directives from their ministers' (Wilpert, cited in Giri 2012: 22). This has meant that 'capitalism continues to get stronger after the adoption of socialism by Chávez' (Giri 2012: 24), and is illustrated by the fact that the share of private sector GDP increased by over 6 per cent between Chávez's election in 1998 and the third quarter of 2008 in spite of nationalizations, in large part because the 'capitalist sector is also benefiting from government spending because it is still dominant, by a long way, in the banking sector, in trade and in the food industry' (Toussaint 2010).

Movements to achieve social change within the state have therefore encountered clear barriers, which can be explained through the reliance of these movements on the views of elites. In turn, this has resulted in the adoption of flexibility and pragmatism in order to negotiate the prevailing political context, an emphasis on only the most immediate problems of capitalism rather than attempts to challenge capitalism itself, and a fundamental acceptance of capitalist rationality (Burnham 2008: 52–3). As such, socialist movements operating within the state, it has been argued, have simply served to play a role in managing the discontent of the labour movement more broadly (ibid.: 54). In this respect, other anti-capitalists have argued that if an alternative to capitalism is to be realized, it must be realized through the state, by revolutionary action to seize state power.

Through the state

Calls to try to realize an alternative to capitalism within the prevailing institutional framework have often not only failed to realize meaningful gains for the socialist movement and failed to stop the ascendancy of capitalism, they have also provoked a considerable critique from revolutionary communists. These anti-capitalists argued that attempts at reform within the existing framework of the state failed to recognize that the state was *a capitalist state*. As a set of institutions that organized the domination of one class by another, they argued, it would be necessary for workers to take state power and use it to dominate the capitalist class up to the point where production for social and civic aims became normalized and it would no longer be necessary to have a force of oppression in the form of the state at all. In failing to recognize this, advocates of achieving change through the seizure of state power argued, advocates of democratic reform within the state had failed to understand fundamental tenets of Marxist theory.

The notion that meaningful social, economic and political change should occur through, as opposed to within, the state emerged alongside those that argued change should occur within the state, and initially took the form of a critique. In response to Eduard Bernstein, Rosa Luxemburg (1900: Introduction) wrote in *Reform or Revolution?* that 'the only factor transforming the entire labour movement from a vain effort to repair the capitalist order into a class struggle against this order, for the suppression of this order – the question: "Reform or Revolution?" as it is posed by Bernstein, equals the question for Social-Democracy: "To be or not to be?"' In other words it was Luxemburg's view that attempts to achieve progress towards socialism within the state represented an abandonment of socialist principles in favour of bourgeois ideas, and as such, she argued that attempts to move towards socialism within the framework of the actually existing state were opportunistic and little more than 'an unconscious attempt to assure predominance of the petty-bourgeois elements that have entered our party' (ibid.: Introduction).

In part, this criticism stemmed from perceptions of cognitive dissonance within Bernstein's own thought. In particular, the notion that capitalism showed a particularly strong ability to adapt to conditions that allowed it to continually reproduce itself meant it was difficult to see how organizations like trade unions and cooperatives could ever be anything more than servicers of capitalism, and much less the 'germs of socialism' (ibid.: ch. I). As such, she noted:

> Revisionist theory thus places itself in a dilemma. Either the socialist transformation is, as was admitted up to now, the consequence of the internal contradictions of capitalism, and with the growth of capitalism will develop its inner contradictions, resulting inevitably at some point in its collapse [...] or the 'means of adaptation' will really stop the collapse of the capitalist system and thereby enable capitalism to maintain itself by suppressing its own contradictions. In that case socialism ceases to be an historical necessity. (Ibid.: ch. I)

The foundation of this critique therefore lies in a theoretical debate about the nature of the crisis dynamic in capitalism. Whereas for revisionists these crisis tendencies could be mediated by pursuing concessions within the institutional framework of the state, for Luxemburg, these crisis tendencies were intrinsic and immutable.

This critique was developed further through a theoretical discussion of the state, which Luxemburg (ibid.: ch. IV) defined as 'an organisation of the ruling class', which comes into conflict with social development as the contradictions of capitalism increasingly express themselves through its crisis-prone development, and the state becomes a class state. Under parliamentarianism, expressions of the interests of society therefore come to take the form of the interests of *capitalist* society because the 'representative institutions, democratic in form, are in content the instruments of the ruling class' (ibid.: ch. IV). This, Luxemburg (ibid.: ch. IV) argued, is manifested in the fact that 'as soon as democracy shows the tendency to negate its class character and become transformed into an instrument of the real interests of the population, the democratic forms are sacrificed'.

In combination, then, Luxemburg's understanding of crisis dynamics in capitalism and the relationship of the state to them suggests that socialist change cannot occur *within* the institutional framework of the capitalist state because this will serve simply to re-create capitalism. As soon as this situation is challenged, she argues, the means through which transition towards an alternative to capitalism are being achieved will be undermined by the state in order to sustain the prevailing capitalist order, thereby negating any gains that had been made on behalf of society more broadly. 'Fourier's scheme of changing [...] the water of all the seas into tasty lemonade was surely a fantastic idea', Luxemburg (ibid.: ch. IV) wrote, but 'proposing to change the sea of capitalist bitterness into a sea of socialist sweetness, by progressively pouring it into bottles of social reformist lemonade, presents an idea that is merely more insipid but no less fantastic'. As such, she argued that 'Only the hammer blow of revolution, that is to say, *the conquest of political power by the proletariat can break down this wall*' (ibid.: ch. IV).

On this basis, there is a clear argument that the only way an alternative to capitalism can be realized is through the state under circumstances where workers struggling against the injustice of capitalist social relations are able to exercise state power. The most famous advocate of effecting change through the state by taking power, Vladimir Lenin, made similar critiques of those advocating reform within the state. For instance, Lenin (1918) argued that Kautsky had 'renounced Marxism by forgetting that *every* state is a machine for the suppression of one class by another, and that the most *democratic* bourgeois republic is a machine for the oppression of the proletariat by the bourgeoisie'. However, the idea that the state is not simply a *capitalist* state, but also a means of oppression, is at the core of Lenin's ideas about the need for the proletariat to take power. Drawing directly on the work of Marx and Engels, Lenin (1904: 7) noted that 'the state is an organ of class rule, an organ for the oppression of one class by another; it is the creation of "order", which legalizes and perpetuates this oppression by moderating the conflict between classes'. The important point of distinction between advocates of reform within the state, and advocates of reform through the state by seizing its power, is that the former view the state as a means of reconciling the antagonism between classes, and the latter view it in terms of its role in perpetuating the subjugation of one class by another.

In light of this perception of the state as an organ of the capitalist class that serves to subjugate the workers through its representation of sectional rather than social interests, it was logically derived that when the state's power is put to the use of society as a whole it would ultimately wither away. As Lenin (ibid.: 12) phrased it, 'When at last [the state] becomes the real representative of the whole of society, it renders itself unnecessary.' Advocates of pursuing change within the framework of the state interpreted Marx and Engels' views on the 'withering away of the state' as suggesting that the need for a violent revolution was unnecessary because as the struggle between classes was increasingly mediated by reform, the state's oppressive functions would also become unnecessary. However, Lenin (ibid.: 12–13) argued that this represented a misreading of Marx and Engels' views on the matter. Rather, he argued that there was an important distinction between the *bourgeois* state and the *proletarian* state. The former, which is the organ of the oppression of the working class by the bourgeoisie, he argued, will continue to be an organ of the bourgeoisie and facilitate the oppression of the working class unless it is abolished because it will continue to represent the interests of that class. Once the bourgeois form of state has been abolished, and replaced with the proletarian form of state, it will become increasingly unnecessary and wither away as it begins to represent social rather than sectional interests.

The argument that the state is an organ for the suppression of one class by another is one element of Lenin's advocacy of reform through the state by seizing its power. A second element lies in the fact that in order to realize its interests, the working class will need the oppressive functions of the state in order to 'suppress the resistance of the exploiters' (ibid.: 17). In the process of 'smashing' bourgeois bureaucracy, conditions are created in which it becomes possible to establish a new bureaucratic machine designed to represent the interests of all of society. Therefore, it is the dual task of anti-capitalists to take state power so they may use the oppressive functions of the state to quash capitalist resistance, and to create a bureaucracy in which the role of officials and civil servants is reduced 'to that of simply carrying out our instructions as responsible, revocable, modestly paid "foremen and accountants"' (ibid.: 30). This form of the state encompasses the notion of the 'dictatorship of the proletariat'.

Like Luxemburg, Lenin (1901: ch. III) therefore argued that trade union politics reduce a broad social struggle to sectional interests within the working classes by emphasizing only the economic struggle. In his discussion of trade union politics, Lenin noted that 'The road to hell is paved with good intentions', but argued that in spite of the good intentions of trade unionism, they 'cannot save one from being spontaneously drawn 'along the line of least resistance' (ibid.: ch. III). It is therefore necessary to encourage the subjugated class – the workers – to see beyond their sectional interests as trade unionists and to recognize their broader class interests, which reflect the fact that capitalism is a form of social organization that is dependent on the exploitation and oppression of one class so that another might benefit. This requires the formation of a revolutionary vanguard, which acts as an advanced contingent in the struggle to seize state power, and replace the bourgeois state with a proletarian state that represents the interests of the whole of society, before it withers away.

Lenin (ibid.: ch. III) argues that this 'Class political consciousness can be brought to the workers *only from without*, that is, only from outside the economic struggle, from outside the sphere of relations between workers and employers.' This is because while it may appear to workers that the struggle in which they are involved is with their employer, these struggles are intrinsic features of a broader political struggle over the coercive ways in which the capitalist state serves to legitimize the separation of workers from the means of production. In order to assist people in recognizing this, Lenin (ibid.: ch. III) argued that it is necessary for the politically aware vanguard to 'go among all classes of the population as theoreticians, as propagandists, as agitators, and as organisers' in order to make people aware of the connection between their individual struggles and the social struggle more broadly, and to organize the action through which state power can be seized, the bourgeois state destroyed, and the proletarian state established through the dictatorship of that class. The role of the intellectual in fostering the conditions for change through the seizure of state power is therefore significant in helping the workers to realize their class consciousness, so that they might overcome their sectional interests.

Calls for anti-capitalism to take place through the state therefore derive from the revolutionary communist movement of the late nineteenth and early twentieth centuries, which argued against the reform of actually existing capitalism and in favour of an immediate transition to an alternative to capitalism. In light of their theory of state, which saw it as an instrument of oppression used by the capitalist class in order to perpetuate the subjugation of workers, they argued that this necessarily involved the seizure of state power. The bourgeois form of the state could therefore be abolished and the dictatorship of the proletariat established to use the oppressive apparatus of the state to serve the interests of all of society rather than simply the capitalist class, until socialism rendered the state itself unnecessary. In order to achieve this, it would be necessary for a vanguard political group to raise the political consciousness of working people above the level of sectional interests, so that they could recognize the nature of capitalist social relations and the state's role in organizing their subjugation, and come to realize the necessity of acting in order to seize state power so that an alternative to capitalism might be created.

Against the state

The notion of seizing state power in order to realize an alternative to capitalism by demolishing the capitalist form of the state and using its oppressive functions to build a proletarian state that serves the interests of all society seems a commonsense form of anti-capitalism. As the state is the organ through which power is most commonly expressed in society, and because anti-capitalism requires a challenge to that power, possession of that power appears to offer a realistic possibility of achieving change. However, the historical experiences of attempts to realize an alternative to capitalism through the state in Russia, China, Cuba and elsewhere have led to widespread criticisms of vanguard parties for their continuing authoritarianism.

The possibility of a revolutionary party taking on the most undesirable characteristics of the capitalist state did not go unnoticed by Lenin himself. He noted how the Russian Revolution of February 1917, in which a provisional government constituted of several different parties replaced Tsar Nicholas II following his abdication from power, quickly began to take the oppressive forms of the old regime. 'Instead of liberty,' Lenin (1917) wrote, 'the old tyranny is coming back.' However, Lenin did not believe that this was a problem inherent in the mode of his anti-capitalism – through the seizure of state power – but in the constitution of the revolutionary forces. He noted how it was 'workers and peasants, the soldiers and sailors, who fought the tsarist troops and shed their blood for liberty' and that 'genuine organisations of the people [...] could and should have taken over state power in full'. However, the majority of the movement's leaders were Socialist-Revolutionaries and Mensheviks, whom Lenin (ibid.) described as 'slaves of the bourgeoisie, shackled by their master'. It was Lenin's view that it was the bourgeois sympathies of these groups which led them to reintroduce the death penalty, disarm workers and arrest and hound other socialist factions (ibid.). Because he believed his party was *truly* socialist, and not a petty bourgeois imitation of a socialist party, he thought it would be possible for it to avoid using state power to oppress the workers, and use it only to oppress the capitalist class so that a proletarian state might be formed to represent the interests of all of society.

In practice, however, the Bolsheviks who replaced the provisional government after the Russian Revolution of October 1917 were 'responsible for restricting and undermining workers' democracy' (Cliff 1959: ch. 7). While Lenin had acknowledged in *The State and Revolution* that it would be necessary for a workers' state government led by the dictatorship of the proletariat to subjugate the interests of the capitalist class in the transition to socialism, even those who had supported the seizure of power in order to realize an alternative to capitalism through the state argued that Leninism went beyond this in practice. As Rosa Luxemburg (1918: ch. VI) noted, 'Freedom only for the supporters of the government, only for the members of one party – however numerous they may be – is no freedom at all.' Because Lenin believed that freedom for the Mensheviks constituted freedom to 'undermine the workers' and peasants' government on behalf of the counterrevolution' (Žižek 2001: 3) he felt that suppression of all dissent was justifiable. However, as Slavoj Žižek (ibid.: 3) has noted, the assumption that the consequences of a person's actions or opinions are objectively known 'closes history', because such opinions are self-reinforcing: 'I decide what your acts objectively mean, since I define the context of a situation (say, if I conceive of my power as the immediate expression of the working class, then every one who opposes me is "objectively" an enemy of the working class)' (ibid.: 3).

Effectively, the Leninist position justified the oppression of different groups of people on the grounds that the party leadership viewed opposition as contrary to their own interests, which they simply asserted were the interests of all of society based on their particular readings of the works of Marx and Engels. As Luxemburg (1918: ch. VI) phrased it, the Bolshevik government became 'at bottom, then, a clique affair – a dictatorship, to be sure, not the dictatorship of the proletariat but only the dictatorship of a handful of politicians'. As such, the practice of Leninist anti-capitalism through the state fully deserved the criticism that it had created a situation in which 'ALL ANIMALS ARE EQUAL BUT SOME ANIMALS ARE MORE EQUAL THAN OTHERS' which was levelled by George Orwell in his literary fable of the Russian revolutionary experience, *Animal Farm* (1987: 90).

The consequences of this form of anti-capitalism did not simply relate to the philosophical concept of freedom, but also had practical implications. Not only was the assumption that the socialist programme was complete an overestimation (Luxemburg 1918: ch. VI), it was also shown that 'every persistent regime of martial law tends inevitably to arbitrariness, and every form of arbitrariness tends to deprave society' (ibid.: ch. VII). In combination, then, the notion of a dictatorship of the proletariat that used the oppressive functions of the state to suppress opposition not only subjugated freedom on the basis of the arguably arbitrary judgements of a party leadership, it also served to militate against the progressive development of a socialist programme and the development of further support for the movement's aims.

Luxemburg (ibid.: ch. VIII) argued that Lenin's anti-capitalism through the seizure of state power repeated the mistakes of reformists, by setting dictatorship and democracy up as oppositional concepts. It was her view that dictatorship should be perceived as 'the *manner of applying democracy*, not in its *elimination*'. This means that the suppression of bourgeois interests must 'proceed step by step out of the active participation of the masses', which is developed through their political education, and not through the views of a small number of bureaucrats that are imposed on society. Luxemburg therefore believed that anti-capitalism should proceed through the seizure of state power, but with this state power being applied through the means of democracy.

In light of historical revolutionary experience and reflection on revolutionary anti-capitalism that suggests 'The world cannot be changed through the state' (Holloway 2005: 19), Holloway (ibid.: ch. 2) has instead argued that anti-capitalism requires the eschewal of power. This is because the act of anti-capitalism and the 'revolutionary transformation of the world' should be perceived as a challenge to the 'very existence of power' and not simply as a challenge to a particularly capitalistic power (ibid.: 17). In other words, it is the aim of anti-capitalism to end the subjugation of all people, which makes the concept of power anachronistic since power is necessarily about subjugation. As such, Holloway (ibid.: 17) argues that 'Once the logic of power is adopted, the struggle against power is already lost.' While Lenin recognized that the state was a capitalist state, he did not recognize that its form could not be fundamentally changed so long as people had to be coerced to engage in certain kinds of social relationships. Anti-capitalist action must therefore recognize the socially constituted nature of existence, and involve the voluntary action of willing participants acting for themselves and their community, rather than the action of a small elite acting on behalf of people and the community.

Holloway describes anti-capitalist action of this nature as a rediscovery and reinvention of the social act of 'doing' (as opposed to the capitalistic act of 'labouring'). This is because 'doing' is necessary for us to meet the needs of our existence, and because a rejection of the capitalistic act of 'labouring', based on the sale of labour-power by the doubly free individual, begins a process of 'negating that which exists' (ibid.: 23) – capitalism. The foundation for this kind of anti-capitalist action, he argues, involves a recognition of the interaction between people that occurs throughout our daily lives and, in particular, recognition of the fact that the commodities we use on a daily basis are not simply commodities, but the products of people's labour, of their 'doing'. It is a central feature of capitalism, according to Holloway, that people's 'power-to-do' is transformed into a 'power-to-labour' through the privatization of the means of production (ibid.: 26–30). It is this which is resisted when we resist capitalism.

Anti-capitalist acts are therefore those that serve to reclaim the social basis of labour through a recognition of the way in which capitalism obscures and denies this social basis; 'The struggle [...] is the struggle to liberate power-to from power-over, the struggle to liberate doing from labour' (ibid.: 36). The principal problem that anti-capitalism encounters is therefore the fetishism of commodities, in which the products of labour come to appear as separate from the labour that produces them through their exchange in a series of monetary transactions. Power therefore lies not in a certain set of institutions such as the state, but the way in which the relations between people come to appear as relationships between things, and in the process subjugates people to the apparent imperatives of the marketplace, and in particular of money. It is 'by showing that these rigidities (money, state, and so on) are merely historically specific forms of social relations, the products of social doing and changeable by social doing', that the practice of anti-capitalism can move us towards an alternative (ibid.: 79). The potential for successful anti-capitalism therefore resides in our realization that we possess power through our ability to act, and are not subject to the power of the things that we create.

In contemporary society, the problem of people's subjugation to the power of things that they create, of money and the state, is particularly problematic because of apparent imperatives of the market and money. As Peter Camejo (1984) has noted, capitalist development has led to the emergence of a feeling that 'while revolutions are possible in the Third World, there is no hope for revolutionary changes within the advanced industrial countries'. He describes this as 'a logic of despair' that 'can influence one to give up on one's own people'. In this situation, he suggests that anti-capitalist action is reduced to the criticism of action by one group of actors by another, which people consider 'involvement in politics' but in actual fact is 'a form of abstention from participation in real living struggles' (ibid.). Anti-capitalist action, he therefore argues, must involve more than critique, which means participation in struggles themselves. For Žižek (ibid.: 3), such calls for anti-capitalists to actively engage in ongoing struggles represent neither a call to 'nostalgically re-enact the "good old revolutionary times" nor opportunistically [and] pragmatically adjust the old program to "new conditions"'. Rather, anti-capitalism is a call to political action and to instigate political projects that can 'undermine the totality of the global liberal-capitalist world order' (ibid.: 3).

The critique of fetishism is therefore not something that can be resolved by a vanguard of intellectuals giving people 'class consciousness'. Rather, fetishism is perceived as a process that is remade through fetishization, and the role of the intellectual in anti-capitalist movements is simply to recognize the way in which capitalism makes sites of contest and struggle such as money, the state and power appear 'fixed phenomena' (Holloway 2005: 90). In this sense, anti-capitalists are not unfetishized individuals in possession of truth, but individuals involved in the struggle against the process of fetishization – that is to say, in the process of doing things differently (ibid.: 105). The revolutionary act of anti-capitalism can therefore be summed up as the 'refusal of domination', of expressing one of the 'million ways of saying No' that people have at their disposal (ibid.: 205).

In a later contribution, Holloway (2010) describes these ways of saying 'No' – the rejection of power – as 'cracking capitalism'. This process begins with a refusal of the social relations that exist; however, this presents a problem because 'If we just fold our arms and do nothing at all, we soon face the problem of starvation' (ibid.: 17). Neither does a simple refusal end the subjugation of one group of people by another, because acts of refusal such as striking suspend the wage relation but do not end it. The act of 'cracking capitalism' therefore begins with a refusal of existing forms of social, economic and political organization, but gains its power when that refusal is complemented by a positive action which is participation in ongoing struggles. Holloway cites examples of workers taking over factories and deciding that they do not need bosses, of teachers taking control of schools in opposition to the marketization of education, as modes of positive action that complement the refusal of what exists (ibid.: 18–19). These actions might stem from 'a conscious opting-out, but they may also result from a forced expulsion from capitalists' social relations' – that is to say, from the contradictory nature of capital's simultaneous dependence on the reproduction and impoverishment of labour in the context of competition and the tendency to engage in accumulation for accumulation's sake (ibid.: 23).

The important distinction to be made between anti-capitalist action against the state, stemming from the refusal of the social relations that exist and doing things differently, and anti-capitalist action within or through the state, is its democratic character. Anti-capitalism through paternalistim and through parliamentary socialism both proceed from the top down, with the views of philanthropists and political elites taken as the marker of a good and just society, and clearly contained the potential to re-create oppressive structures. Leninist anti-capitalism through the state, through its recognition of the state's nature as an instrument of oppression and its intention to use it to oppress an oppressing class, also assumes the normative desirability of the creation of a socialist commonwealth held by a small group of people who would pursue it on behalf of others. As such, the top-down approach of anti-capitalism within and through the state relies in both cases on assumptions about the desirability of a particular form of social, political and economic organization, which have the clear potential to become oppressive when 'taken seriously as a model for how society should be organised' because deviations from the model require subjugation (ibid.: 38). In contrast, the anti-capitalist tradition against the state 'is characterised by respect for all those involved, the promotion of active participation, direct democracy and comradeship' (ibid.: 40). In other words, anti-capitalist action against the state is action that begins from the rejection of the social relations that exist and involves the acceptance of a plurality of views that can account for the individualism of people. It is clear that these acts of resistance themselves do not offer a fatal blow to capitalism, but what matters is not 'purity' of ideas, but the struggle against capitalism itself (ibid.: 58).

By rejecting the idea that anti-capitalists need to seize state power in order to effect change on the grounds that anti-capitalism is concerned with a struggle against power, anti-capitalism against the state has two clear benefits. First, it rejects the philosophical and practical problems of freedom associated with one group of people pursuing change on behalf of another, since it rejects the possibility that a post-capitalist future can be planned, and avoids the compromises and conflicts that have historically stemmed from the disagreement between leaders of anti-capitalist movements and society more broadly conceived. In other words, it avoids the problems of paternalism associated with some forms of anti-capitalism within the state, and the problem of subjugation associated with anti-capitalism through the state. In the process, anti-capitalism against the state serves to avoid creating divisions among different factions of anti-capitalists who each perceive their own alternative and their own method to be 'correct', and all others to be an indication of the co-option of other anti-capitalists by the bourgeoisie. As Peter Camejo (1984) phrased it, 'If an atmosphere tolerant of differences and debate does not exist among revolutionaries, they will find it difficult to respond to changing conditions or to correct errors' and 'More often than not, two "vanguards" each calling the other "petty bourgeoisie", emerge.'

Secondly, anti-capitalism against the state transforms the struggle against capitalism from a niche activity, in which small groups of activists are involved, into something that is participatory, and includes any action that refuses participation in the act of labouring in favour of a social (as opposed to monetary) action. As such, anti-capitalism against the state can also avoid problems that might stem from the exclusive nature of 'movements', which tend towards judgements of anti-capitalist action in terms of 'the numbers game; this many demonstrators, that much damage' (Leeds May Day Group 2008: 116). While the individual action might not appear to have a great deal of impact on capitalist social relations as a whole, the sum of many individual actions can be far more profound: 'I refuse to go to work and instead sit in a park reading a book: this is a pleasure that requires no justification; but if everyone else decides to do the same thing, then capitalism will collapse' (Holloway 2010: 73). The idea of anti-capitalist action that resists the state's power as a form of capitalist social relations therefore responds to the principal problem of alternatives to capitalism raised in Chapter 3, because it emphasizes the social constitution of capitalism and its alternatives. That is to say, capitalism is not something that exists but is constantly remade or resisted in our everyday actions, and an alternative to capitalism would not be something that represented an outcome to be realized, because it would be necessary to continue to act against capitalism and the inequalities it produces in order to ensure that alternatives do not degenerate and that any oppressive relations carried over from a previous form of social organization or inadvertently created by new forms can be ironed out. The desirability of this form of anti-capitalism can be practically emphasized in the following terms, which highlight the historical evolution of our interests and perceptions of justice and equality:

> A program written in 1984, as opposed to one written in 1954, would include a different spectrum of questions, though many fundamental considerations would remain the same. Issues that have evolved – or, where our understanding has evolved – include the oppression of women, the treatment of homosexuals, problems related to pollution and the environment, the development of new sectors of the working class, and the tasks facing oppressed nationalities. (Camejo 1984)

The Zapatista movement of the Chiapas region of Mexico can be regarded as an exemplary example of this form of anti-capitalism against the state – as Abigail Andrews (2010: 91) suggests, the 'global left has elevated them as a paradigm of radical politics and transnational solidarity'. In its early days the movement was open to 'vertical' support relationships, which involved 'expansively encouraging Northerners to come to Chiapas' (ibid.: 102), and suggested a degree of dependence on capitalist interests. However, this situation often resulted in outsiders determining the form and content of support, and ultimately led to 'Regular donations of cast off goods' such as a 'single pink stiletto heel as "humanitarian aid"', which symbolized a lack of respect for the movement (ibid.: 103) and necessitated the transformation of the relationship between the movement and its supporters. As the movement has developed, the Zapatistas have been able to reverse this relationship so that although they remain dependent on the support of others to achieve their aims, they 'now impose their own demands on supporters rather than the reverse' (ibid.: 99). This means that supporters' proposals for donations and development projects are subject to the approval of the Zapatistas' deliberative processes, which have increasingly come to be accepted by those offering support from the outside (ibid.: 99–100).

The Zapatistas' experience suggests that the pursuit of basic social rights by local populations organized collectively can resist being co-opted by outside interests, even where they might be dependent on those outside interests for support. Through the establishment of 'horizontal' support networks of this kind, the Zapatista councils have been able to continue overseeing programmes of relevance to their local communities, including in the areas of education and healthcare, within the framework of a broader struggle against the encroachments of capital, which was clearly manifested in the adoption of the North American Free Trade Agreement and catalysed the movement's formation in 1994. Anti-capitalism against the state in this form therefore recognizes the social constitution of reality, and the necessity of treating the world we live in (or wish to live in) as a process that requires constant responses to the intended and unintended consequences of the way we interact with each other. It therefore not only recognizes that the state is a *capitalist* state, but also recognizes that it is a capitalist state because it is in itself a form of capitalist *social relations*.

Challenges for anti-capitalism

The notion of anti-capitalist action occurring against the state is therefore able to account for problems posed by the state's existence as a form of capitalist social relations, and offers a pluralistic and inclusive way of practising anti-capitalism. This is because it begins from the proposition that the world in which we live is constituted through our social action, and recognizes that it can be resisted through our social action, and must continually be remade by our social action if society is to adapt in a positive way to changing social and historical contexts. In the process, its pluralism avoids the pitfalls of paternalism and co-option that have often characterized anti-capitalism within the state and the pitfall of oppression that has characterized anti-capitalism through the state.

The practice of anti-capitalism against the state nonetheless faces two potential barriers. The first relates to the problem of developing broad awareness of the fact that capitalism itself is not immutable, and that there is more than one way to live one's life with authenticity. However, in the contemporary world we are besieged by the pervasive notion that there are things that we 'must' do in order to be good citizens; we 'must' engage in the capitalist labour market and contribute to international competitiveness; we 'must' develop our skills in accordance with the demands of capitalism in order to achieve this. These ideas are entrenched in policies like welfare conditionality that make the discipline of starvation that operates through the doubly free nature of labour under capitalist social relations more acute. The idea that we 'must' contribute to the development of capitalism is further entrenched by structures that prioritize certain kinds of employment over others, and which is manifested in the United Kingdom in the fact that universities are ranked according to (among other things) the proportion of their students in professional and managerial positions and graduate salaries twelve months after graduation. The quality of a good education, in other words, can be judged by the extent to which that education creates good capitalists.

Politically, these decisions are justified by treating participation in the economy as politically neutral facts – through the depoliticization of economic policy-making. That is to say, governments argue that they have no alternative but to grant central banks independence to control inflation, whatever the consequences for levels of employment, because the demands of international bond markets leave them with no alternative (Burnham 2001). It is argued that globalization has meant that governments are forced to minimize levels of corporate taxation and social expenditure in order to attract capital investment, which, as Matthew Watson and Colin Hay (2003) have argued, is a means of rendering contingent decisions necessary decisions. Both examples and more besides are tied up with the immutability of competition and the way it has developed over time to constrain states.

Psychologically, individuals are asked to justify these outcomes by seeing them as opportunities:

> the ruling ideology endeavours to sell us the very insecurity caused by the dismantling of the Welfare State as an opportunity for new freedoms. You have to change jobs every year, relying on short-term contracts instead of a long-term, stable appointment. Why not see it as liberation from the constraints of a fixed job, as the chance to reinvent yourself again and again, to become aware of and realize the hidden potentials of your personality? (Žižek 2001: 4)

Although capitalist social relations do not formally remove our ability to do things differently – to engage in anti-capitalism against the state – in practice they contain implicit disciplinary structures that encourage our participation. As Žižek (ibid.: 5) notes, even in instances when people have the explicit freedom to do something, they tend to make the same decisions as those implicitly denied it, by rationalizing their decision to act according to prevailing norms. Jon Elster (1989b: 138–9) explains this empirically in terms of people's tendencies not to undertake anti-capitalist actions (which he describes as pursuing self-realization) because they cannot 'bring themselves to undergo the painful learning process that is required' or because they see the status quo as a lower risk than an attempt at change. In an environment in which people perceive few opportunities for self-realization, he suggests people's 'desires and aspirations might unconsciously adjust to this limitation to avoid cognitive dissonance' (ibid.: 155).

The extent to which the state is involved in arguing that there are *in reality* few opportunities to do things differently, and uses rhetoric and institutional arrangements to reinforce this perception, are demonstrations of the fact that the state is a *capitalist* state. However, it is also possible to see how the arguments deployed to justify this action are constructions; there has never been a time in which capitalist states sought to be uncompetitive or to implement policies that were not credible (Bonefeld 2008b); capital has never been 'national' because social relations are mediated by money which in principle deterritorializes economic relations (Holloway 2005; Ingham 1996). Through the recognition of these things, the possibility of realizing an alternative form of social relationships becomes a more realistic prospect.

The first challenge for anti-capitalism therefore lies in spreading the idea that there is an alternative way of living our lives, and that we have the power to realize it because the world is continually made and remade through our social action. J. K. Gibson-Graham (2003: 126) has described this as a 'challenge to the unfreedom' that generates and entrenches a reluctance to engage in economic experimentation. One way in which this could be achieved is through the education system, with its potential to reach many people. However, given the state's nature as a form of capitalist social relations, the prospect of state funded education being used as a forum for teaching alternatives seems remote. As such, if anti-capitalist action is to gain momentum, it is likely to do so by developing connections between anti-capitalist activities that already exist. As Harry Cleaver (2008) has noted, many such means already exist, and as 'a general rule the wider and deeper the linkages [between anti-capitalist struggles], the more successful struggles have been, the greater the isolation, the more likely the defeat' (ibid.: 129). Cleaver develops analogies of networks, rhizomes, and currents in order to characterize the way in which these linkages might successfully be developed; however, the most significant point is that the practice of anti-capitalism must attempt to link the autonomous anti-capitalist actions of differing groups to create a plurality of alternative social practices if it is to expand the spaces in which they can flourish. It is here that the 'horizontal' network-building of the Zapatista movement (Andrews 2010) can be taken as an indication of the possibilities for realizing and developing an alternative to capitalism that exist.

Conclusions

This chapter has argued that, by virtue of its social constitution, the state *is a capitalist state.* In other words, because the institutions of the state are forms of interaction between people and the predominant mode of interaction between people is capitalist, for as long as those relations remain capitalist, the state will serve to reproduce those social relationships. By drawing on historical debates about reform versus revolution, the chapter argued that focusing on sectional interests served to divert attention from the struggle against capitalism more broadly, and that attempts to seize state power by revolutionary vanguards have served to reproduce exploitative power relations. The notion that there is some kind of objective truth about the ideal form that social relationships should take relies on problematic foundations in the sense that it necessitates one group of people asserting the best interests of another. More worryingly, it has historically led to the suppression of alternative views in the name of this general interest. It is clear that the suppression of the wishes of others in the name of the general good has the potential to be oppressive and stifling for human well-being by facilitating subjugation of people that is equal to or worse than that prevailing under the current form of capitalism.

In order to avoid such a scenario it is necessary that anti-capitalist principles be inclusive and democratic, open to the varying forms of social and economic organization that might exist. The practice of anti-capitalism, more significantly, must be willing to engage with experimentation rather than prescriptive plans so that reflection on practice can serve to minimize the possibility that emerging forms of social and economic organization serve to re-create relationships of oppression and subjugation. Critics of this mode of anti-capitalism might argue that small-scale, 'bottom-up' action offers only a remote possibility of success given the pervasive nature of the capitalist economy. They might ask, 'How could the actions of individuals or small groups of individuals possibly lead us to an alternative to capitalism?' The intuitive answer is that the capitalist behemoth will submerge alternative spaces and show anti-capitalism of this form to be a hopeless task. However, there is a hopeful answer to this question stemming from our recognition of the social constitution of state, economy and society; we know for certain that if we do not take action to do things differently we will not realize an alternative future. Through action, we do not simply have the ability to change the world, we actually change it; the experience of the Zapatistas demonstrates this. In recognizing this, the realization of an alternative to capitalism becomes something more than a figment of our imaginations, the incentive to attempt such actions is increased, and the chances of achieving change are greatly magnified.

CONCLUSIONS: FROM HERE TO THERE?

The aim of this book has been to examine what is meant by capitalism, what the implications of capitalism are, what alternatives to it might exist, and how they might be realized. Its central argument has been based on the notion that capitalism and its alternatives are forms of social relationships – that is, reflections of the way that people interact with one another on a day-to-day basis. As such, the way in which the consequences of capitalism are understood shapes whether it is perceived to be a desirable or flawed system of social organization, as well as perceptions of the merits of alternative capitalisms or alternatives to capitalism. Furthermore, the recognition that prevailing social and economic systems are socially constituted also presents a clear possibility for people to resist capitalism rather than remake it, through engagement and experimentation with alternative forms of social action. The core argument that this book has made, therefore, is that capitalism is not an immutable form of social organization with a logic that cannot be resisted, and alternatives to capitalism are not outcomes to be achieved once and for all. Instead, it has suggested that capitalism and its alternatives are social forms that are made and continually remade or resisted through our everyday actions, and which must continually be remade if social action is to produce outcomes that do not degenerate into capitalism or reproduce its injustices.

The first chapter introduced capitalism as it has been understood by Adam Smith, Karl Marx, John Maynard Keynes and Friedrich Hayek. It demonstrated that each of these political economists had differing views about the way in which wealth was created in the economy, and discussed the implications that their particular views had for the way in which the relationship between the state and the market should be organized in an ideal sense. In doing so, the chapter showed that the way in which the core concept of wealth and the social activities that create and distribute wealth are understood are extremely significant for our judgements about the desirability of capitalism, the desirability and basis for an alternative (to) capitalism, and the extent to which we should engage in the practice of anti-capitalism to resist the prevailing form of social relationships. For instance, liberals drawing on Smith who believe that the division of labour creates wealth and produces benefits that can be realized by everybody if the state creates conditions in which trade can flourish will come to very different conclusions to Marxists, who believe that the creation of wealth is dependent on the separation of one class of people from the means of subsistence, and forces them to sell their labour-power so that a small class of people might benefit at their expense. Likewise, a Keynesian who believes that capitalism shows a tendency towards sustained periods of depression that requires state intervention to offset saving, which stems from people's uncertainty about the future, will come to very different conclusions about capitalism to a neoliberal, who believes that competition and the price system are the only efficient ways of coordinating economic behaviour in a market system.

The second chapter then related the relationship between state and market imagined by Smith, Keynes and Hayek to the forms of state that prevailed in the interwar, post-war and post-1979 periods, before examining historical crises of capitalism associated with them. It showed how each of these different forms of governing capitalist social relations – through the laissez-faire liberal, Keynesian and neoliberal state forms – failed to provide for economic and social stability, and therefore argued that the forms of state imagined by Smith, Keynes and Hayek have not appeared to be able to provide a practical basis for stability in capitalist social relations. For instance, it noted how the Gold Standard had deflationary consequences that increased pressure on states for social reform, as well as exacerbating problems of international competitiveness, and how speculation in the 1920s created property and stock market bubbles that proved unsustainable. In combination, these events amplified the conflict between social well-being and capital accumulation, resulting in beggar-thy-neighbour policies between states that deepened the Great Depression. In response to these events, the embedded liberal compromise of the post-war period drew on Keynesian political economy and attempted to create a framework in which states could intervene in the employment market to respond to social pressures, but was progressively undermined by evolutions in global finance, the increasing power of labour movements, and the inflationary consequences of the OPEC price increases. Ultimately, the simultaneous occurrence of rising inflation and rising unemployment undermined the legitimacy of embedded liberalism and the Keynesian state form, as monetarism and neoliberalism became established as the dominant intellectual paradigms. As marketization became established as the norm in the 1980s, the chapter suggested the rise of financialization in the wake of welfare state retrenchment led to a divorce of the productive and financial economies; as speculation on the basis of assumptions about the ability of people to manage risk (as opposed to uncertainty) ultimately proved to be unfounded, the neoliberal form of capitalist social relations resulted in the Great Recession, and further fiscal policy retrenchment as states responded to perceived problems of sovereign debt. In light of the historical recurrence of crises in capitalism manifested in the crises of the laissez-faire liberal, Keynesian and neoliberal state forms, the chapter argued – drawing on Marx – that capitalism is, *in itself, an inherently crisis-prone form of social relationships.* It argued that this crisis tendency stems from the contradiction that lies in capitalism's dependence on the reproduction of labour in order to produce and consume commodities, and its simultaneous need to reduce wages and replace living labour with machinery in the context of competition, and the tendency to engage in accumulation for accumulation's sake.

Through its discussion of historical and theoretical tendencies towards crises, Chapter 2 argued that there is a strong rationale for an alternative to capitalism. While it argued that capitalism itself was inherently crisis-prone, Chapter 3 began by considering the fact that it may simply be the prevailing *form* of capitalism which is crisis-prone, and that this tendency towards crisis originates in the fact that the state has always persistently intervened in the economy to a greater or lesser degree. As such, it discussed the philosophical position of libertarians who have argued that the only state intervention that can be perceived as legitimate on the grounds of social justice is acting to protect property rights and individual liberty. Extrapolating from the work of Hayek, the chapter discussed how this form of libertarian capitalism relies on the notion that markets tend towards equilibrium, and the abstract assumption that it could be reconciled with social justice in a way that would result in long-term stability. However, in light of the fact that attempts to reconcile freedom with equality within this framework rely on abstract theoretical constructions, the chapter argued that such an organizing system is unlikely to be stable over the long run because social tensions would be likely to mount in the face of rising inequality. It then outlined cooperative and socialist alternatives to capitalism, and showed how each responded to the crisis dynamics outlined in Chapter 2 by elevating the importance of social and civic aims relative to the aim of profit-seeking, and argued that they had the potential to mitigate crisis dynamics in capitalism. However, it also showed how historical experiences of cooperative economies demonstrate a tendency for them to degenerate over time, how the socialization of the means of production has not always resulted in long-run social benefits, and how the socialist movement itself has tended to reproduce certain undesirable social relations of capitalism, such as gender inequality. On this basis, the chapter argued that any alternative (to) capitalism should not be thought of as a desirable outcome of social action, but rather as a process that must be continually remade if it is not simply to degenerate into or reproduce forms of social relationships that are deemed to be undesirable. In other words, there is not one 'correct' alternative to capitalism, but many.

Chapter 4 then addressed the question of anti-capitalism, asking how it might be possible for an alternative to capitalism to be realized. It began by arguing that the state is a form of prevailing social relationships, and that as these are predominantly capitalist, the state should be thought of as a capitalist state that attempts to mediate the antagonisms between capital and labour (the crisis tendencies of capitalist social relations). It then discussed the possibility of achieving change within the state, through attempts to create cooperatives funded by philanthropy, and parliamentary socialism. It suggested that because both of these forms of anti-capitalism operate with a 'top-down' dynamic, which relies on economic and political elites pursuing social interests on behalf of the majority, paternalism and parliamentary socialism are prone to co-option by capitalist interests, which results respectively in a tendency towards cooperative decline and parliamentary conservatism. The chapter then showed how nineteenth- and twentieth-century revolutionaries like Luxemburg and Lenin argued instead that change should be brought about by seizing state power so that representatives of the working classes could use the coercive instruments at the state's disposal in order to suppress the capitalist class until a socialist commonwealth was created. When this was achieved, the state could pursue the interests of all of society rather than the interests of one class, before ultimately withering away. However, it also showed how historical experience has shown this mode of anti-capitalism to be oppressive, as dissenting voices become labelled as anti-progressive or petty bourgeois, which has stifled debate and provoked discontent as people's freedom of expression is curtailed. Finally, it discussed John Holloway's notion that anti-capitalist action should occur against the state, which begins with the rejection of the prevailing form of social relationships, combined with social action that rejects the capitalistic act of labour in favour of the social act of 'doing'. The chapter argued that the grassroots foundations of such an approach to anti-capitalism, along with its pluralistic basis, represents a form of anti-capitalism that recognizes the social constitution of the state, economy and society, and avoids the accusations of paternalism and oppression that have been levelled at other forms of anti-capitalism. While it does not prescribe a programme for what an alternative to capitalism might look like, the approach is an optimistic and realistic one because of its recognition that the world in which we live can be changed through our actions. As such, the chapter argued that anti-capitalist actions should be democratic, diverse and experimental.

From here to there/What is to be done?

In addition to emphasizing the social constitution of economy and society and introducing key theories in political economy, historical crises in capitalism, forms that an alternative (to) capitalism might take, and theories of anti-capitalism, the book has made a number of substantive arguments in the chapters summarized above, which require further reflection. First, it has argued that capitalism is an inherently crisis-prone form of social relations, and that an alternative to capitalism would be desirable. Secondly, it has argued that this alternative should take a form that places a greater significance on social and civic objectives than on pecuniary gain, but cannot be prescribed without succumbing to the problems of degeneration, or reproducing or relying on capitalist forms of oppression and subjugation. Finally, it suggested that attempts to realize alternatives to capitalism – anti-capitalism – should proceed from the 'bottom up' through engagement in and experimentation with alternative forms of production, distribution and exchange.

These substantive arguments raise issues that are familiar to discussions of capitalism, its alternatives and anti-capitalism, and have often taken the form of the statement 'From here to there' or the question 'What is to be done?' While the debate over reform versus revolution implicitly suggests a programme of action geared towards achieving a particular outcome – which in historical terms has often been a form of cooperative economy or a socialist commonwealth – this book has argued, following Holloway, that it is the rejection of social relationships that experience suggests are exploitative and crisis-prone, through engagement with alternative forms of social action, which is important. Furthermore, it has argued that thinking of an alternative (to) capitalism as an outcome to be realized once and for all does not adequately recognize the fact that economy and society are constantly made and remade through our social action, and must constantly be made and remade in order to avoid the degeneration of an alternative over time, or reproducing or creating relationships that are unjust.

In making this argument, the book has consciously sought to acknowledge that reasonable people might disagree about how far it is capitalism itself which is the source of injustice and crises. At its most general level, then, the book has emphasized the significance of careful reflection on the nature of the world in which we live, the implications of how it is organized for economic stability and social justice, and the importance of coming to a judgement about how this fits with the kind of world in which we would like to live. In other words, the book has ultimately argued that the process of meaningful change begins from a consideration of how we perceive capitalism; it has asked the reader to consider at what point things such as poverty and environmental degradation should stop being treated as side effects, and at what point crises should stop being treated as anomalies, in an otherwise desirable system. If, on considered reflection, this point has been reached, and these things become viewed as malignancies of capitalism, a rationale for an alternative has been established.

More specifically, the book's reflection on these questions themselves, through its discussion of the nature of historical crises of capitalism and the apparent tendency towards crises within capitalism, has been able to build an argument for an alternative to capitalism on the basis of a robust empirical critique of different historical forms of capitalism. However, while the book ultimately rejected a libertarian alternative capitalism, it has also acknowledged that cooperative and socialist alternatives are not the only potential futures beyond the prevailing form of neoliberal capitalism, and has also guarded against the idea that any alternative form of social organization represents a palliative for the problems of capitalism. Rather, it has emphasized the notion that social outcomes stem from our social action, and so it is from continued reflection on the consequences of our social action that a more just and stable future can emerge. In addressing the issues 'From here to there' and 'What is to be done?', it is tempting to look for a programme of action with predetermined steps that can be used to realize the desired alternative, but experience has shown that a framework in which groups of people act on behalf of other people or 'people in general' will tend to compromise the interests and/or stifle the freedoms of those who are being 'represented'. As such, anti-capitalist action should be pluralistic, inclusive and experimental. We need to form statements and ask questions not in the common form of 'From here to there' or 'What is to be done?', because both imply an end-point to be realized, and which this book has shown creates a tendency towards the re-creation of oppressive structures of capitalism itself. Instead, we need to realize that there is no single 'there', which recognizes the inherently crisis-prone nature of capitalism in its acceptance of the desirability of change, the possibility of alternatives that stem from the social constitution of state economy and society, and, most significantly, the importance of pluralism in our thinking about forms of economic organization and the means by which we attempt to realize them.

How do we begin to move, then, from here to any of the varying forms that an alternative to capitalism might take? First, we must reflect very carefully about what the implications of the way in which wealth is created and used in capitalism are. Secondly, we must recognize that the world we live in is socially constituted, and the notions that 'there is no alternative' or that people or governments 'must' act in certain ways are rhetorical constructions. If the injustices, contradictions and crisis-prone tendencies of capitalism are recognized, we can then begin to organize relations of production, distribution and exchange on a different basis. Clearly, given the scale of capitalism and its power, this is not an easy task. However, because capitalism is something people have created by interacting with each other according to certain norms, there is no reason why it can't be unmade, and an alternative developed, by challenging those norms with new forms of social activity.

REFERENCES

Andrews, A. (2010) 'Constructing mutuality: the Zapatistas' transformation of transnational power dynamics', *Latin American Politics and Society*, 52(1): 89–120.

Andrews, D. M. (1994) 'Capital mobility and state autonomy: toward a structural theory of international monetary relations', *International Studies Quarterly*, 38(3): 193–218.

Balardini, F. (2012) 'The self-destructive logic of capitalism and the Occupy movement', *Socialism and Democracy*, 26(2): 35–8.

Ball, R. J. and T. Burns (1976) 'The inflationary mechanism in the UK economy', *American Economic Review*, 66(4): 467–84.

Balls, E. (1998) 'Open macroeconomics in an open economy', *Scottish Journal of Political Economy*, 45(2): 113–32.

Barrow, C. W. (2008) 'Ralph Miliband and the instrumentalist theory of the state: the (mis)construction of an analytic concept', in P. Wetherly, C. Barrow and P. Burnham (eds), *Class, Power and the State in Capitalist Society: Essays on Ralph Miliband*, Basingstoke: Palgrave Macmillan, pp. 84–108.

Baylis, S., S. Smith and P. Owens (eds) (2011) *The Globalization of World Politics: An Introduction to International Relations*, Oxford: OUP.

Becker, M. (2007) 'World Social Forum', *Peace & Change*, 32(2): 203–20.

Beechey, V. (1977) 'Some notes on female wage labour in capitalist production', *Capital & Class*, 1(3): 45–66.

Bergsten, C. F. (2005) *The United States and the World Economy: Foreign Economic Policy for the Next Decade*, Washington, DC: Institute for International Economics.

Bernanke, B. and H. James (1991) 'The Gold Standard, deflation and financial crisis in the Great Depression: an international comparison', in R. G. Hubbard (ed.), *Financial Markets and Financial Crises*, Chicago, IL: University of Chicago Press, pp. 33–68.

Bernstein, E. (1899) *Evolutionary Socialism*, Preface, www.marxists.org/reference/archive/bernstein/works/1899/evsoc/preface.htm, accessed 1 September 2013.

Biagiotti, I. (2004) 'The World Social Forums. A paradoxical application of participatory doctrine', *International Social Science Journal*, 56(182): 529–40.

Bienefeld, M. (1992) 'Financial deregulation: disarming the nation state', *Studies in Political Economy*, 37(1): 31–59.

Blaug, M. (1997) *Economic Theory in Retrospect*, 5th edn, Cambridge: Cambridge University Press.

Block, F. (1987) *Revisiting State Theory: Essays in Politics and Post-Industrialism*, Philadelphia: Temple University Press.

Boltanski, L. (2002) 'The left after May 1968 and the longing for total revolution', *Thesis Eleven*, 69(1): 1–20.

Bonefeld, W. (1992) 'Social constitution and the form of the capitalist state', in W. Bonefeld, R. Gunn and

K. Psychopedis (eds), *Open Marxism*, vol I: *Dialectics and History*, London: Pluto, pp. 93–132.

— (2008a) 'Subverting the present, imagining the future: insurrection, movement, commons', in W. Bonefeld (ed.), *Subverting the Present, Imagining the Future: Insurrection, Movement, Commons*, New York: Autonmedia, pp. 7–12.

— (2008b) 'Global capital, national state, and the international', *Critique*, 36(1): 63–72.

Booth, A. (1983) 'The Keynesian revolution in economic policy-making', *Economic History Review*, New Series, 36(1): 103–23.

Boydston, B. D. (2010) 'What exactly does the Occupy movement want?', *The Humanist*, 72(1): 20–3.

Broadberry, S. and N. Crafts (2001) 'Competition and innovation in 1950s Britain', *Business History*, 43(1): 97–118.

Bryson, V. (2004) 'Marxism and feminism: can the "unhappy marriage" be saved?', *Journal of Political Ideologies*, 9(1): 13–30.

BSA (2009) 'Converting failed financial institutions into mutual organisations', Report from the Oxford Centre for Mutual and Employee-owned Business, Kellogg College, Oxford, Building Societies Association, economics.ouls.ox.ac.uk/15197/1/ Converting_financial_institutions_ into_mutual_organisations_-_final. pdf, accessed 1 September 2013.

— (2013a) *Building Societies Key Statistics*, Building Societies Association, www.bsa.org.uk/keystats/index.htm, accessed 1 September 2013.

— (2013b) *Mortgage Market Share Summary*, Building Societies Association, www.bsa.org.uk/docs/statisticspdfs/ mortgages/mortgage_market_share_ summary.pdf, accessed 1 September 2013.

Burk, K. and A. Cairncross (1992) *'Goodbye, Great Britain': The 1976 IMF Crisis*, New Haven, CT: Yale University Press.

Burke, E. (1774) *Speech to the Electors of Bristol*, press-pubs.uchicago.edu/ founders/documents/v1ch13s7.html, accessed 1 September 2013.

Burnham, P. (1994) 'The organisational view of the state', *Politics*, 14(1): 1–7.

— (1995) 'Capital, crisis and the international state system', in W. Bonefeld and J. Holloway (eds), *Global Capital, National State and the Politics of Money*, Basingstoke: Macmillan, pp. 92–115.

— (1999) 'The politics of economic management in the 1990s', *New Political Economy*, 4(1): 37–54.

— (2001) 'New Labour and the politics of depoliticisation', *British Journal of Politics and International Relations*, 3(2): 127–49.

— (2003) *Remaking the Postwar World Economy: Operation Robot and British Policy in the 1950s*, Basingstoke: Palgrave Macmillan.

— (2008) 'Parliamentary socialism, Labourism and beyond', in P. Wetherly, C. W. Barrow and P. Burnham (eds), *Class, Power, and the State in Capitalist Society*, Basingstoke: Palgrave Macmillan, pp. 48–63.

— (2011) 'Towards a political theory of crisis: policy and resistance across Europe', *New Political Science*, 33(4): 493–507.

Camejo, Peter (1984) *Problems of Vanguardism: In Defense of Leninism*, www.marxists.org/archive/ camejo/1984/19841001.htm, accessed 1 September 2013.

CAP (2013) 'Fiscal austerity is undermining long-term U.S. economic prospects', Center for American Progress, www.americanprogress.org/issues/ economy/news/2013/06/06/64608/

fiscal-austerity-is-undermining-long-term-u-s-economic-prospects/, accessed 28 August 2013.

Carter, N. (2006) 'Political participation and the workplace: the Spillover Thesis revisited', *British Journal of Politics and International Relations*, 8(4): 410–26.

Cerny, P. G. (1991) 'The limits of deregulation: transnational interpenetration and policy change', *European Journal of Political Research*, 19(2/3): 173–96.

— (1997) 'Paradoxes of the competition state: the dynamics of political globalization', *Government & Opposition*, 32(2): 251–74.

Challis, C. E. (1967) 'The debasement of the coinage, 1542–1551', *Economic History Review*, New Series, 20(3): 441–66.

Chang, H. (2010) *23 Things They Don't Tell You about Capitalism*, New York: Bloomsbury.

Childs, D. (1979) *Britain since 1945: A Political History*, London: Ernest Benn Ltd.

Chomsky, N. (2012) *Occupy*, London: Penguin.

Clarke, P. (2004) *Hope and Glory: Britain 1900–2000*, 2nd edn, London: Penguin.

Clarke, S. (2001) 'The globalisation of capital, crisis and class struggle', *Capital & Class*, 75: 93–101.

— (2011 [1988]) *Keynesianism, Monetarism, and the Crisis of the State*, Kindle edn.

— (2011 [1982]) *Marx, Marginalism, and Modern Sociology*, Kindle edn (originally Basingstoke: Macmillan).

Cleaver, H. (2008) 'Deep currents rising: some notes on the global challenge to capitalism', in W. Bonefeld (ed.), *Subverting the Present, Imagining the Future: Insurrection, Movement, Commons*, New York: Autonmedia, pp. 122–60.

Cliff, T. (1959) *Rosa Luxemburg*, ch. 7, www.marxists.org/archive/cliff/works/1959/rosalux/7-bolpower.htm, accessed 12 November 2013.

Coates, D. (1975) *The Labour Party and the Struggle for Socialism*, Cambridge: Cambridge University Press.

Cohen, B. J. (1996) 'Phoenix risen: the resurrection of global finance', *World Politics*, 48(2): 268–98.

— (1998) *The Geography of Money*, Ithaca, NY: Cornell University Press.

Cohen, G. A. (1982) 'The structure of proletarian unfreedom', *Philosophy & Public Affairs*, 12(1): 3–33.

— (1985) 'Nozick on appropriation', *New Left Review*, I(150): 89–105.

— (1986) 'Self-ownership, world ownership and equality: Part II', *Social Philosophy & Policy*, 3(2): 77–96.

— (2000) 'If you're an egalitarian, how come you're so rich?', *Journal of Ethics*, 4(1/2): 1–26.

— (2009) *Why Not Socialism?*, Princeton, NJ: Princeton University Press.

Cornwell, J. (2012) 'Worker co-operatives and spaces of possibility: an investigation of subject space at collective copies', *Antipode*, 44(3): 725–44.

Crouch, C. (2009) 'Privatised Keynesianism: an unacknowledged policy regime', *British Journal of Politics and International Relations*, 11(3): 382–99.

CSE Sex and Class Group (1982) 'Sex and class', *Capital & Class*, 16: 78–94.

Cuninghame, P. (2008) 'Reinventing an/other anti-capitalism in Mexico: the Sixth Declaration of the EZLN and the "Other Campaign"', in W. Bonefeld (ed.), *Subverting the Present, Imagining the Future: Insurrection, Movement, Commons*, New York: Autonmedia, pp. 203–30.

Cunliffe, J. and A. Reeve (1996) 'Exploitation: the original St Simonian account', *Capital & Class*, 59: 61–80.

Day, J. P. (1966) 'Locke on property', *Philosophical Quarterly*, 64: 207–20.

De Goede, M. (2004) 'Repoliticizing financial risk', *Economy and Society*, 33(2): 197–217.

De Sousa Santos, B. (2008) 'The World Social Forum and the global left', *Politics & Society*, 36(2): 247–70.

De Vries, M. G. (1985) *The International Monetary Fund 1973–1978: Cooperation on Trial*, vol. I, Washington, DC; International Monetary Fund.

— (1986) *The IMF in a Changing World*, Washington, DC: International Monetary Fund.

Deeg, R. and M. A. O'Sullivan (2009) 'The political economy of global finance capital', *World Politics*, 61(4): 731–63.

Dintenfass, M. (1992) *The Decline of Industrial Britain 1870–1990*, London: Routledge.

Drury, S. B. (1982) 'Locke and Nozick on property', *Political Studies*, 30(1): 28–41.

Dumenil, G. and D. Levy (2001) 'Costs and benefits of neoliberalism: a class analysis', *Review of International Political Economy*, 8(4): 578–607.

Dworkin, R. (1981) 'What is equality? Part 2: Equality of resources', *Philosophy & Public Affairs*, 10(4): 283–345.

Eichengreen, B. (1996) *Globalizing Capital: A History of the International Monetary System*, Princeton, NJ: Princeton University Press.

Elias, J. (2006) 'Stitching-up the labour market: recruitment, gender and ethnicity in the multinational firm', *International Feminist Journal of Politics*, 7(1): 90–111.

Elster, J. (1989a) 'From here to there; or, if cooperative ownership is so desirable, why are there so few cooperatives?', *Social Philosophy & Policy*, 6(2): 93–111.

— (1989b) 'Self-realisation in work and politics: the Marxist conception of the good life', in J. Elster and K. O. Moene (eds), *Alternatives to Capitalism*, Cambridge: Cambridge University Press, pp. 127–58.

Engels, F. (1908) *Socialism: Utopian and Scientific*, Chicago, IL: Charles H. Kerr (scanned from the original and reprinted in the Forgotten Books Series).

— (2004 [1884]) *The Origin of the Family, Private Property and the State*, Introduction by P. Brewer, New South Wales: Resistance Books, readingfromtheleft.com/PDF/EngelsOrigin.pdf, accessed 18 July 2013.

Eurostat (2013) 'Euro area unemployment rate at 12.2%', Eurostat news release 102/2013, May, epp.eurostat.ec.europa.eu/cache/ity_public/3-01072013-bp/en/3-01072013-bp-en.pdf, accessed 29 July 2013.

Evans, P. (1997) 'The eclipse of the state? Reflections on stateness in an era of globalization', *World Politics*, 50(1): 62–87.

Felkerson, J. (2011) '$29,000,000,000,000: a detailed look at the Fed's bailout by funding facility and recipient', Working Paper 698, Levy Economics Institute of Baird College.

Fine, B. and A. Saad-Filho (2010) *Marx's Capital*, 5th edn, London: Pluto.

Finlayson, A. (2009) 'Financialisation, financial literacy and asset-based welfare', *British Journal of Politics and International Relations*, 11(3): 400–21.

Fontanel, J., J.-P. Herbert and I. Sampson (2008) 'The birth of political economy or the economy in the heart of politics: mercantilism', *Defence and Peace Economics*, 19(5): 331–8.

Friedman, M. (1975) *Unemployment versus Inflation: An Evaluation of the Phillips Curve*, Occasional Paper no. 44, London: Institute for Economic Affairs.

— (1976) *Inflation and Unemployment: The New Dimension of Politics*, Occasional Paper no. 51, London: Institute for Economic Affairs.

Galbraith, J. K. (2009 [1955]) *The Great Crash 1929*, London: Penguin.

Gamble, A. (1995) 'The new political economy', *Political Studies*, XLIII: 516–30.

— (1996a) 'Hayek and the left', *Political Quarterly*, 67(1): 46–53.

— (1996b) *Hayek: The Iron Cage of Liberty*, Cambridge: Polity.

— (2001) 'Neo-liberalism', *Capital & Class*, 25: 127–33.

— (2009) *The Spectre at the Feast: Capitalist Crisis and the Politics of Recession*, Basingstoke: Palgrave.

Gamson, W. A. and M. L. Sifry (2013) 'The #Occupy movement: an introduction', *Sociological Quarterly*, 54: 159–63.

Gibson-Graham, J. K. (2003) 'Enabling ethical economies: cooperativism and class', *Critical Sociology*, 29(2): 123–61.

Gill, S. and D. Law (1989) 'Global hegemony and the structural power of capital', *International Studies Quarterly*, 33(4): 475–99.

Giri, S. (2012) 'Capitalism expands but the discourse is radicalized: whither "21st century Venezuelan socialism"?', *Critical Sociology*, 31(1): 21–36.

Goldstein, L. F. (1982) 'Early feminist themes in French utopian socialism: the St Simonians-and Fourier', *Journal of the History of Ideas*, 43(1): 91–108.

Goodwin, B. (1978) *Social Science and Utopia*, Sussex: Harvester Press.

Grant, W. (2002) *Economic Policy in Britain*, Basingstoke: Palgrave Macmillan.

Hall, P. A. (1993) 'Policy paradigms, social learning and the state', *Comparative Politics*, 25(3): 275–96.

Harrison, J. C. F. (1969) *Robert Owen and the Owenites in Britain and America: The Quest for the New Moral World*, London: Routledge & Kegan Paul.

Hartmann, H. (1979) 'The unhappy marriage of Marxism and feminism: towards a more progressive union', *Capital & Class*, 8: 1–34.

Harvey, D. (2006) *The Limits to Capital*, revised edn, London: Verso.

Hawthorne, M. (1939) 'Hawthorne and utopian socialism', *New England Quarterly*, 12(4): 726–30.

Hay, C. (2001) 'Negotiating international constraints: the antinomies of credibility and competitiveness in the political economy of New Labour', *Competition and Change*, 5(3): 269–89.

— (2004) 'Credibility, competitiveness and the business cycle in "Third Way" political economy: a critical evaluation of economic policy in Britain since 1997', *New Political Economy*, 9(1): 39–56.

— (2007) *Why We Hate Politics*, Cambridge: Polity.

Hayek, F. A. (1937) 'Economics and knowledge', *Economica*, New Series, 13: 33–54.

— (1945) 'The use of knowledge in society', *American Economic Review*, 35(4): 519–30.

— (2001 [1945]) *The Road to Serfdom*, Reader's Digest condensed edn, London: Institute for Economic Affairs.

Heilbroner, R. (2000) *The Worldly Philosophers: The Lives, Times and Ideas of the Great Economic Thinkers*, revised 7th edn, London: Penguin.

Hesse, H. and M. Cihak (2007) 'Cooperative banks and financial stability', IMF Working Paper WP/07/07, Washington, DC: International Monetary Fund.

Holloway, J. (1992) 'Crisis, fetishism, class composition', in W. Bonefeld, R. Gunn and K. Psychopedis (eds),

Open Marxism, vol. II: *Theory and Practice*, London: Pluto, pp. 145–69.

— (1995) 'The abyss opens: the rise and fall of Keynesianism', in W. Bonefeld and J. Holloway (eds), *Global Capital, National State, and the Politics of Money*, Basingstoke, Palgrave Macmillan, pp. 7–34.

— (2005) *Change the World without Taking Power: The Meaning of Revolution Today*, revised edn, London: Pluto.

— (2010) *Crack Capitalism*, London: Pluto.

Humphries, J. (1983) 'The "emancipation" of women in the 1970s and 1980s: from the latent to the floating', *Capital & Class*, 20: 6–28.

Ingham, G. (1996) 'Money is a social relation', *Review of Social Economy*, 54(4): 507–29.

International Monetary Fund (2012) 'France: financial system stability assessment', IMF Country Report no. 12/341, Washington, DC: International Monetary Fund, www.imf.org/external /pubs/ft/scr/2012/cr12341.pdf.

Jarsulic, M. (2010) *The Anatomy of a Financial Crisis*, Basingstoke: Palgrave Macmillan.

Jessop, B. (1990) *State Theory: Putting the Capitalist State in Its Place*, Cambridge: Polity.

— (2001) 'State theory, regulation and autopoiesis: debates and controversies', *Capital & Class*, 75: 83–92.

— (2008) 'Dialogue of the deaf: some reflections on the Poulantzas Miliband debate', in P. Wetherly, C. Barrow and P. Burnham (eds), *Class, Power and the State in Capitalist Society: Essays on Ralph Miliband*, Basingstoke: Palgrave Macmillan, pp. 132–57.

Kautsky, K. (1918) *The Dictatorship of the Proletariat*, www.marxists.org/archive/kautsky/1918/dictprole/ch02.htm, accessed 1 September 2013.

Kennemore, A. and G. Weeks (2011) 'Twenty-first century socialism? The elusive search for a post-neoliberal development model in Bolivia and Ecuador', *Bulletin of Latin American Research*, 30(2): 267–81.

Kettell, S. (2004) *The Political Economy of Exchange Rate Policy-Making: From the Gold Standard to the Euro*, Basingstoke: Palgrave Macmillan.

Keynes, J. M. (1924) *A Tract on Monetary Reform*, London: Macmillan & Co., 203.200.22.249:8080/jspui/bitstream/123456789/2209/1/A_tract_on_monetary_reform.pdf, accessed 1 September 2013.

— (1930) *Economic Possibilities for Our Grandchildren*, www.econ.yale.edu/smith/econ116a/keynes1.pdf, accessed 30 November 2012.

— (1937) 'The General Theory of Employment', *Quarterly Journal of Economics*, 51(2): 209–23.

— (2008 [1936]) *The General Theory of Employment, Interest, and Money*, California: BN Publishing.

Klein, N. (2011) 'Occupy Wall Street: the most important thing in the world right now', *Critical Quarterly*, 54(2): 1–4.

Krueger, A. O. (1998) 'Whither the World Bank and the IMF', *Journal of Economic Literature*, 36(4): 1983–2020.

Laidler, D. E. W. (1975) *The End of Demand Management: How to Reduce Unemployment in the 1970s*, Occasional Paper no. 44, London: Institute for Economic Affairs.

— (1976) 'Inflation in Britain: a monetarist perspective', *American Economic Review*, 66(4): 485–500.

Lairson, T. D. and D. Skidmore (2003) *International Political Economy: The Struggle for Power and Wealth*, Belmont, CA: Wadsworth.

Larkin, C. (2006) 'The Great Re-coinage of 1696: developments in monetary theory', Working Paper, Trinity College Dublin, www.atl-res.com/finance/LARKIN2.pdf, accessed 22 October 2012.

Laski, H. J. (1931) *The Limitations of the Expert*, London: Fabian Society.

Leeds May Day Group (2008) 'Anti-capitalist movements', in W. Bonefeld (ed.), *Subverting the Present, Imagining the Future: Insurrection, Movement, Commons*, New York: Autonomedia.

Lenin, V. I. (1901) *What is to be Done?*, ch. III, www.marxists.org/archive/lenin/works/1901/witbd/iii.htm, accessed 1 September 2013.

— (1904) *The State and Revolution: The Marxist Theory of the State and the Tasks of the Proletariat in the Revolution*, www.marxists.org/ebooks/lenin/state-and-revolution.pdf, accessed 1 September 2013.

— (1913) 'The three sources and three component parts of Marxism', www.marxists.org/archive/lenin/works/1913/mar/x01.htm, accessed 1 September 2013.

— (1917) *Lessons of the Revolution*, www.marxists.org/archive/lenin/works/1917/sep/06.htm, accessed 1 September 2013.

— (1918) *The Proletarian Revolution and the Renegade Kautsky*, www.marxists.org/archive/lenin/works/1918/oct/10.htm, accessed 1 September 2013.

Leopold, D. (2005) 'The structure of Marx and Engels' considered account of utopian socialism', *History of Political Thought*, 26(3): 443–66.

Locke, J. (1764 [1689]) *Two Treatises of Government*, London: A. Miller et al., files.libertyfund.org/files/222/0057_Bk.pdf, accessed 15 November 2013.

Löwy, M. (2002) 'The revolutionary romanticism of May 1968', *Thesis Eleven*, 68(1): 95–100.

Ludlam, S. (1992) 'The Gnomes of Washington: four myths of the 1976 IMF crisis', *Political Studies*, 40(4): 713–27.

Luxemburg, R. (1900) *Reform or Revolution?*, www.marxists.org/archive/luxemburg/1900/reform-revolution/intro.htm, accessed 1 September 2013.

— (1918) *The Russian Revolution*, www.marxists.org/archive/luxemburg/1918/russian-revolution/cho6.htm, accessed 1 September 2013.

Malinov, M. (2013) 'Occupy at one year: growing the roots of a movement', *Sociological Quarterly*, 54: 206–313.

Marx, K. (1858) *Grundrisse*, Notebook VI, www.marxists.org/archive/marx/works/1857/grundrisse/ch12.htm, accessed 1 September 2013.

— (1990 [1867]) *Capital: A Critique of Political Economy*, vol. I, introduced by Ernest Mandel, translated by Ben Fowkes, London: Penguin.

Marx, K. and F. Engels (1985 [1848]) *The Communist Manifesto*, ed. with an introduction by A. J. P. Taylor, London: Penguin.

Matthews, R. C. (1968) 'Why has Britain had full employment since the war?', *Economic Journal*, 311: 555–69.

McKinnon, R. I. (1992) 'Spontaneous order on the road back from socialism: an Asian perspective', *American Economic Review*, 82(2): 31–6.

Miliband, R. (1970) 'The capitalist state: reply to Nicos Poulantzas', *New Left Review*, 59: 53–60.

— (1972) *Parliamentary Socialism*, revised edn, London: Merlin Press.

Miller, D. (1981) 'Market neutrality and the failure of co-operatives', *British Journal of Political Science*, 11(3): 309–29.

Moggridge, D. E. (1969) *The Return to Gold, 1925*, Cambridge: Cambridge University Press.

Nogues-Marco, P. (2011) 'The microeconomics of bullionism: arbitrage, smuggling and silver outflows in Spain in the early 18th century', Working Papers in Economic History, WP 11-05, Carlos III University, Madrid, e-archivo.uc3m.es/bitstream/10016/11425/1/wp%20 11-05.pdf, accessed 22 October 2012.

Nozick, R. (1974) *Anarchy, State and Utopia*, Oxford: Blackwell.

O'Brien, P. K. (1987) 'Britain's economy between the wars: a survey of the counter revolution in economic history', *Past and Present*, 115: 105–30.

O'Brien, R. and M. Williams (2010) *Global Political Economy*, 3rd edn, Basingstoke: Palgrave Macmillan.

Occupy Wall Street (2011) 'Declaration of the Occupation of New York City', www.nycga.net/resources/documents/declaration/, accessed 19 November 2013.

Orwell, G. (1987) *Animal Farm*, London: Penguin.

Otsuka, M. (2003) *Libertarianism without Inequality*, Oxford: Oxford University Press.

Owen, R. (1991) *A New View of Society and Other Writings*, ed. with an introduction by G. Claeys, London: Penguin.

Plender, J. (1986) 'London's Big Bang in international context', *International Affairs*, 63(1): 39–48.

Polanyi, K. (2001 [1944]) *The Great Transformation: The Political and Economic Origins of Our Time*, Boston, MA: Beacon Press.

Poulantzas, N. (1969) 'The problem of the capitalist state', *New Left Review*, 58: 67–78.

Rawls, J. (1985) 'Justice as fairness: political not metaphysical', *Philosophy & Public Affairs*, 14(3): 223–51.

Rice, T. (1993) 'Demand curves, economists, and desert islands: a response to Feldman and Dowd', *Journal of Health Economics*, 12(2): 201–4.

Rogers, C. (2009) 'From Social Contract to "Social Contrick": the depoliticisation of economic policy-making under Harold Wilson, 1974–75', *British Journal of Politics and International Relations*, 11(4): 634–51.

— (2012) *The IMF and European Economies: Crisis and Conditionality*, Basingstoke: Palgrave Macmillan.

— (2013) 'Crisis, ideas, and economic policy-making in Britain during the 1970s stagflation', *New Political Economy*, 18(1): 1–20.

Ruggie, J. G. (1982) 'International regimes, transactions, and change: embedded liberalism in the postwar economic order', *International Organization*, 36(2): 379–415.

Sargant, W. L. (2005 [1860]) *Robert Owen and His Social Philosophy*, Elibron Classics.

Schumpeter, J. (2010 [1943]) *Capitalism, Socialism and Democracy*, London: Routledge.

Schwartz, H. (2008) 'Housing, global finance, and American hegemony: building conservative politics one brick at a time', *Comparative European Politics*, 6(2): 262–84.

Shukaitis, S. (2008) 'Dancing amidst the flames: imagination and self-organization in a minor key', in W. Bonefeld (ed.), *Subverting the Present, Imagining the Future: Insurrection, Movement, Commons*, New York: Autonmedia, pp. 99–115.

Skeet, I. (1988) *Opec: Twenty Five Years of Prices and Politics*, Cambridge: Cambridge University Press.

Skidelsky, R. (2010) *Keynes: The Return of The Master*, revised and updated edn, London: Penguin.

Smith, A. (1776) *The Wealth of Nations*, Kindle edn.

Stilwell, F. (2012) *Political Economy: The Contest of Economic Ideas*, 3rd edn, Oxford: Oxford University Press.

Subramaniam, K. (2011) 'Lessons from the financial crisis: failure of markets or failure of regulation', *Macroeconomics and Finance in Emerging Market Economies*, 4(2): 343–9.

Sullivan, O. (2000) 'The division of domestic labour: twenty years of change?', *Sociology*, 34(3): 437–56.

Tomlinson, J. (1981) 'Why was there never a "Keynesian revolution" in economic policy?', *Economy and Society*, 10(1): 72–87.

— (1984) 'A "Keynesian revolution: in economic policy?"', *Economic History Review*, 37(2): 258–62.

— (1990) *Public Policy and the Economy since 1900*, Oxford: Clarendon Press.

Tormey, S. (2004) *Anti-Capitalism: A Beginner's Guide*, Oxford: OneWorld.

Toussaint, E. (2010) 'The Venezuelan economy: in transition towards socialism?', Part III, Committee for the Abolition of Third World Debt, cadtm.org/The-Venezuelan-economy-in, accessed 19 November 2013.

Triffin, R. (1969) 'The thrust of history in international monetary reform', *Foreign Affairs*, 47(3): 477–92.

Viner, J. (1930) 'English theories of foreign trade before Adam Smith', *Journal of Political Economy*, 38(3): 249–301.

Warde, A. and K. Hetherington (1993) 'A changing domestic division of labour? Issues of measurement and interpretation', *Work, Employment and Society*, 7(1): 23–45.

Watson, M. (2005) *Foundations of International Political Economy*, Basingstoke: Palgrave Macmillan.

— (2012) 'Friedrich List's Adam Smith historiography and the contested origins of development theory', *Third World Quarterly*, 33(3): 459–74.

Watson, M. and C. Hay (2003) 'The discourse of globalisation and the logic of No Alternative: rendering the contingent necessary in the political economy of New Labour', *Policy and Politics*, 31(3): 289–305.

Watts, M. (2001) '1968 and all that ...', *Progress in Human Geography*, 25(2): 157–88.

West, E. G. (1969) 'The political economy of alienation: Karl Marx and Adam Smith', *Oxford Economic Papers*, New Series, 21(1): 1–23.

Widmaier, W. W., M. Blyth and L. Seabrooke (2007) 'Exogenous shocks or endogenous constructions? The meanings of wars and crises', *International Studies Quarterly*, 51(4): 747–59.

World Social Forum (2013) 'World Social Forum Charter of Principles', www.fsm2013.org/en/node/204, accessed 29 July 2013.

Wright, E. O. (2010) *Envisaging Real Utopias*, London: Verso.

Zizek, S. (2001) 'What can Lenin tell us about freedom today?', *Rethinking Marxism: A Journal of Economics, Culture & Society*, 13(2): 1–9.

INDEX

www.ingramcontent.com/pod-product-compliance
Ingram Content Group UK Ltd.
Pitfield, Milton Keynes, MK11 3LW, UK
UKHW040741020325
455689UK00002B/14